BEING THE BEST

The Nonprofit Organization's
Guide to Total Quality

Frederick A. Lambert, Ed.D.

Copyright © 2014 Frederick A. Lambert, Ed.D.

Author photo by Neal Warren

All rights reserved. No part of this book may be used or reproduced by any means, graphic, electronic, or mechanical, including photocopying, recording, taping or by any information storage retrieval system without the written permission of the publisher except in the case of brief quotations embodied in critical articles and reviews.

Abbott Press books may be ordered through booksellers or by contacting:

Abbott Press
1663 Liberty Drive
Bloomington, IN 47403
www.abbottpress.com
Phone: 1-866-697-5310

Because of the dynamic nature of the Internet, any web addresses or links contained in this book may have changed since publication and may no longer be valid. The views expressed in this work are solely those of the author and do not necessarily reflect the views of the publisher, and the publisher hereby disclaims any responsibility for them.

Any people depicted in stock imagery provided by Thinkstock are models, and such images are being used for illustrative purposes only. Certain stock imagery © Thinkstock.

ISBN: 978-1-4582-1348-8 (sc)
ISBN: 978-1-4582-1347-1 (hc)
ISBN: 978-1-4582-1346-4 (e)

Library of Congress Control Number: 2013923442

Printed in the United States of America.

Abbott Press rev. date: 1/21/2014

To Julie
With Love
ALWAYS

CONTENTS

Preface vii

Chapter 1: Quality: Foundation of Success 1
Chapter 2: Nonprofit's Triple Bottom Line 7
Chapter 3: Strategic Plan: Blueprint For Success 23
Chapter 4: Board & Staff: A Partnership for Quality 41
Chapter 5: Creating & Sustaining a Culture of Quality ... 67
Chapter 6: The Customer: First, Foremost & Always 93
Chapter 7: Measurement: Quality's Assurance 107
Chapter 8: Leadership: Transforming Theory to
Reality 127

Appendices

1. SWOT Analysis Sample 155
2. SWOT Analysis Cover Letter Sample 157
3. Board Assessment Instrument 159
4. Candidate Assessment Form 161
5. Candidate Finalist Rating System 162
6. Needs Assessment Template 163
7. Customer Satisfaction Template 164

Bibliography 165

PREFACE

At the conclusion of a strategic planning board retreat that I facilitated, one of the board members approached me and indicated that he found the session very interesting, but of little use, since the organization for which the retreat was run was a nonprofit. The board member continued by saying that while the theories and practices that were presented and suggested would work for a "business", they had no application for a nonprofit. This episode disturbed me a great deal. I wondered how many other board members and boards thought the same way. Thus, the idea for this book was born.

At the outset a word about my background might be helpful. I have spent the 45 years of my professional life in the nonprofit world, initially, higher education in which I served as a member of the undergraduate and graduate faculty, as well as, a University Dean. For the 15 years prior to my retirement in 2005, I served as the President of a major arts organization. Since retiring I have served nonprofits as a consultant specializing in strategic planning, systems analysis and design, staff and board development. Throughout my professional life

I have served on boards of social service, education, arts, and religious nonprofit organizations.

When I left the world of the "academy" I wondered if the theories that I had studied and taught about management and leadership would really "work". I am happy to report they did! It wasn't always easy to influence the board, and more especially, long tenured associates, but the increased success and organizational growth that was realized served as compelling evidence that the hard work involved in managing the organization as a "business" worked. Every theory, and more importantly, every application contained in this book has been tried and has worked.

The book uses the theories and practices of Total Quality Management (TQM) as the operational framework for the organizational transformation required to develop and sustain increased organizational growth and success. The theoretical base is laced with practical suggestions for the design, implementation and assessment of systems whose goal it is to continuously improve the organization.

One of the challenges I faced in writing the book was the realization that there wasn't one simple model that fit all nonprofits. There were differences of type, size, scope, governance, organizational structure and culture. While there was a moment of temptation to limit the audience, upon reflection, I believed that was too restrictive. Every attempt has been made to offer practical suggestions that would have universal application, understanding that based on the nature and mission of the specific organization, some of the iterations may be more complex in their application and adoption.

The originally intended audience for the book was board members and key organizational leaders. Again, after reflection, that audience needed to widen, so that nonprofit organizations' staff, volunteers, and other stakeholders could understand their roles in the transformational process, thereby preparing them to lend ready and enthusiastic support for organizational change.

The book is designed to follow an organizational development sequence. It would lend itself easily as background and a framework for staff development programs and leadership retreats. Minimally, board officers, the organization's chief executive or operations officer, and department heads would benefit from a reading and subsequent reflection and discussion of the book's contents.

The board member to whom I referred at the beginning was correct in one thing. Nonprofit organizations are different from a for profit business. Nonprofits serve a public interest and cannot declare a traditional profit to be shared with its shareholders. But, these technical differences do not render nonprofit organizations any less worthy of being lead and managed with the same expertise and sophistication as their for profit counterparts. The case could actually be made that because of the significance of the nonprofits' role and community impact, nonprofit organizations have more need and responsibility to run themselves according to sound business practices, thus safeguarding and securing the noble and significant contributions nonprofits provide.

It is hoped that this book can in some measure enhance the quality of nonprofit organizations to serve their noble missions with passion, to inspire their leadership and associates to act with integrity and creativity, and to encourage their stakeholders to offer generous and enthusiastic support. Through this collaboration of energy and commitment nonprofit organizations will indeed engage in the "business" of BEING THE BEST!

FAL/November, 2013

CHAPTER 1

Quality: Foundation of Success

Principles of Total Quality Management

For the past ninety years successful organizations have subscribed to some or all of the principles espoused in Total Quality Management (TQM). Most of these organizations have been for profit and many in the manufacturing sector. Indeed, it was for these organizations and within them that the theories were devised and in which they have been best and most often practiced.

Over the past twenty five years the base of the world's economy changed from the predominance of the manufacturing sector to the service sector. Many areas of the world have seen the disappearance of manufacturing firms in favor of technology companies and the growth of service industries, such as, hospitality, entertainment, education, retail, health and social services.

At the same time traditional nonprofits (501)(c)(3) have struggled for survival, and some have not prevailed. We read and hear monthly of symphonies that have either reduced their offerings or folded. Museums have reduced staff, programming and visiting hours. Arts organizations have competed for new audiences; some sacrificing their mission to "win the battle". Social service agencies have competed for diminishing government, corporate and philanthropic resources. Nonprofit boards and staff in attempts to address the situation have hired consultants, merged with other organizations, and downsized; all in the name of survival.

This book is written as an attempt to address the very real challenges facing the (501)(c)(3) nonprofit organizations. It posits that the principles of total quality management, which were designed for the manufacturing sector of the last century, have relevance and significance for the nonprofit today. It further takes the position that the solutions to many of the contemporary challenges nonprofits face can be found in the tenets and practices of total quality management.

At the outset it is appropriate to summarize the operational principles that drive a total quality management approach.

First and foremost, the preeminence of a focus on the customer/client and her/his needs is essential to an organization's quality performance. All systems are designed to meet and exceed these needs and to make it easy and pleasurable for the customer/client to approach the organization and to benefit from its services and offerings. Ken Blanchard (2007) in his work, Leading at a Higher Level, refers to this as an organization's "relentless focus on customer service." It is the main objective of a quality organization to engage the customer/client in a long term positive relationship. Some management theorists have actually said that the goal of a quality organization is to create *"delighted customers"*.

Some within non-profit organizations resist this total customer focus because they believe that in order for the organization to accomplish this customer focus the organization has to subscribe to the adage: "the customer is always right." Especially in education and health care this concept is looked upon with suspicion, because the service deliverers believe they have knowledge or skills that the customer/client lacks. This indeed may be the case, but the principle of a customer/client focus doesn't imply that the knowledge and skills don't exist or that they are to be put aside, but rather that in their delivery the recipient of the service or offering is treated as valued, important and ultimately "delighted".

Customer focus informs all of the other principles and practices; hence, is essential. It often requires a systemic restructuring to ensure that all facets of the organization are equally committed to the customer/client orientation and the quality delivery of the organization's services and offerings.

The second principle governing a quality organization is the concept of *continuous improvement.* Simply put, an organization that commits to quality management can never be satisfied that what service it offers and how the service is delivered is perfect, and therefore not in need of any improvement. Often this aspect is frustrated by a chorus of "we've always done it this way". Rather, today's success is but preamble to tomorrow's new or improved service or its revised or improved delivery. This function should not be relegated to a particular department to oversee, but rather be ingrained in the corporate culture, for while there are technical aspects to the process; it is an attitudinal characteristic.

In addition to the attitudinal support of the organization's associates and leadership, continuous improvement requires systemic support in terms of developing, implementing, and monitoring a *process* driven by the customer focus.

The same customer focus that benefits the external user applies, as well, to the internal customers: the associates and organization's leadership. In such an environment, information flows openly and regularly with a goal of rendering the associates as engaged employees. It is only by such practices that the common development of a culture of quality caring in the delivery of services can exist. With the exception of personnel matters, there are no compelling reasons why all other information cannot be shared with everyone in the organization, thereby creating an engaged partnership to develop and sustain the process of continuous improvement.

The cultural aspects of continuous improvement drive the quality process, but the improvement process needs to be equally supported and directed by a consistent assessment of the services delivered and a sharing of the data with the associates. Based upon these data, decisions can be made to change either delivery systems or the services delivered.

Change is a constant in an organization truly committed to continuous improvement. Not everyone is comfortable in such an environment, but if the connection to customer satisfaction is made and those associates most engaged in the development and delivery of services are involved in the process, change can actually be a liberating and enhancing experience for the associates and the harbinger of the organization's quality performance and its ultimate success.

Organizations committed to the principles of customer satisfaction and continuous improvement support these goals structurally by the development of operational teams. Ideally, these teams should be interdisciplinary or cross functional. Membership on cross functional teams is determined by who in the organization has information that is critical to a decision and who will ultimately be most impacted by the decision.

Formal reporting arrangements are abandoned in favor of a sharing of knowledge. The quality of the decisions these teams make is directly relational to the people who constitute the team. Such a structure allows for the easy and regular flow of information that has been cited earlier as essential to the continuous improvement process.

For these teams to be effective, and not just an administrative restructuring, they need to be truly empowered to make decisions and implement them. Such "ownership" is at the foundation of a quality organization and needs to be valued and rewarded as such.

The organization's internal administrative arrangements should be designed to energize the internal customers (the associates) and to make it easy for them to do their jobs well and to deliver services efficiently and effectively to the external customers/clients.

Earlier reference was made to the assessment of services and its relationship to continuous improvement. The quantifiable results of such assessment form the basis for all decisions within an organization committed to quality. And, these decisions are best made by those closest to the customer/client, not executives, senior management or boards.

It is important that decisions, especially those that call for changes to the organization's structure, its delivery systems, or the services delivered be based on fact and not any individual's or group's hunch, or worse, whim. Quantitative analysis will ensure that these decisions have objective bases for implementation and improved customer satisfaction as their goal. An open sharing of the data will also facilitate organizational support for any changes proposed.

Obviously, the organizational transformation that an adoption of and a commitment to these principles requires the organization's leadership to consistently think and act with a strategic focus on long term success. This coupled with the constant espousal of the organization's mission and a systems approach to the organization's operation, will provide the direction and support needed to develop and sustain a quality organization.

CHAPTER 2

Nonprofit's Triple Bottom Line

The Nature of a Nonprofit Organization

It is important to understand what is meant by a "nonprofit organization". Put in the simplest terms, and as non-technically as possible, a nonprofit organization is one that has been granted a tax exempt status based on its mission to serve as an organization in the *public interest*. The organization therefore more than likely serves the public interest as a charitable, educational, scientific, religious or literary organization.

The nonprofit does not declare a profit, but rather uses any operating surplus in the service of the public interest for which it is designed. Its corporate structure designated by the IRS as a (501)(c)(3) is similar to a for profit organization in many ways, with the exception that the nonprofit has no shareholders. The nonprofit organization is exempt from federal, most State and local taxes. The nonprofit's employees however are subject to all Federal, State and local taxes. This legal definition of the organization's tax status does not mean that it cannot have clients/customers; that it can't charge for its services; that it doesn't have to market itself and its services; and, that it shouldn't raise money to supplement fee for service revenue. It is only through the successful growth of these functions that the organization will compete with similar providers and excel as a quality organization.

As has been stated above, the nonprofit organization cannot declare a profit, which in the for profit world is the financial statement's "bottom line": How much money was made for the organization's shareholders? Instead, because of its nature as an organization serving the public interest, the nonprofit has three bottom lines: fulfillment of mission; client/customer recruitment and service; and adequate return on its human and financial investments to sustain the organization and its commitment to continuous improvement.

The Organization's Mission

Nonprofit organizations are founded to meet a public need. The organization's purpose is to be found in its mission. There is no document that is more important to an organization's long term success than its mission. Its aspirations should be a motivating force for all engaged in the process of leading the organization and those who develop and deliver its services. Effective mission statements therefore of their nature should be simple statements of what service is to be offered, to what population, to what level of level of quality. From the mission statement flows the organization's vision and core values statements. To render its foundational nature operative, the mission statement should be written in simple, but inspirational language. It should not exceed one page and its essential points can be remembered by anyone after one reading.

One key function of an effective mission statement is the differentiation of the organization from organizations of a similar nature. This *distinctive competency* often is difficult to develop and state, but the process to do so will render great returns in terms of specifying what the organization does well and for whom. The iteration should simply state what is unique or special about the organization in order to differentiate it from others.

Too many mission statements fail the *simplicity test*, especially those describing educational and religious institutions. These tend to be so filled with complex pedagogical, philosophical or theological concepts that the essential message is lost or obscured. The length of these statements often does not encourage even those involved with the organization to want to read them. How motivating can such documents be?

Mission statements form the bases for all quality management efforts within the organization and therefore need to be clear in their statements about function, client/customer base, standards of excellence and distinctive competency. These four categories will serve as the foundation for all the organization's activities and the bases for the ultimate measure of its success. The clearer and simpler the document is written; the easier it can be accessed and understood. The frequency of its public reference will determine its viability.

An organization's mission does not usually change over the long term. But, at the same time, it should be revisited annually by the organization's leadership to ensure that the need for the service for which the organization has been founded is still current; the number of people served warrants the efforts expended; and, that the quality of the service delivery exceeds the clients'/customers' expectations. In this way the mission continues to be the vibrant, living document it needs to be: one that inspires and directs everything that the organization does and the level of quality at which it aims to perform.

None of the above is intended to indicate that a revision in the organization's mission may not be needed based on the assessment of its fulfillment over time. A vibrant organization, committed to total quality, will regularly assess factors external to the organization, as well as, how the essential mission is being fulfilled. If the external assessment yields significant changes in the population, the extreme duplication of services, or similar organizations that deliver the same service better, the organization's leadership should explore a tweaking of the mission to allow it to describe what the organization does best. The assessment may also encourage the organization to engage in client/customer development activities to attract new populations.

It is often difficult for organizations that have existed for the better part of a century or longer to admit that the "times have changed" and that the service offered by the organization may no longer have the same audience it once did, thus rendering the organization's offerings/ services no longer needed, desirable or relevant. Such an honest assessment should be coupled with the courage to close the organization or seek to merge with another similar organization. If the steps outlined regarding the development and the assessment of the mission are conducted annually, such an extreme, dire situation should not occur.

More often there is a greater challenge that arises for the organization's leadership and associates when there is a service or offering that doesn't specifically meet mission, but can be lucrative. Engaging in such activities can have short term benefit in terms of the dollars earned, but begins an erosion process to the organization's prime purpose and can easily slip into a "downward spiral" leading to the organization's extinction. Certainly with major donors, especially foundations, such a move away from mission can have a negative impact on their level of support.

This is not to imply in any way that organizations cannot develop and try new ventures designed specifically to attract new populations. The key is to ensure that these are developed with the purpose also of fulfilling and extending mission. Such efforts at creativity are often met with "but we've never done that before". Any organization that allows such naysaying attitudes to exist unchecked, is dooming itself to potential irrelevance and possible extinction. An organization has to adapt to changing times, especially with regard to the changing demographics: the population served, and the competition. Again, as long as the intention of these new initiatives is to fulfill and expand mission, they should be encouraged and be seen as a "lifeline" for the organization's sustainability and long term success.

The mission's role as the primary bottom line will be further developed in later chapters dealing with strategic planning and program / service assessment.

The Organization's Customers

The nature of the nonprofit organization and the basis for its tax exempt status flows from the reason for its existence: to serve the *public interest*. This rationale implies that there is a "public" to be served and it is solely for its "interest" that the organization exists. Therefore, the organizations must have clients, students, parishioners, audiences, patients to serve in order to justify its existence and fulfill its mission. For the sake of simplicity, these will all be referred to as customers throughout the book. Further, the preeminent position the customer has within quality management theory, renders it essential to any discussion on quality. Therefore its place in the triple bottom line.

The difficulty some organizations may have with this concept has been acknowledged earlier. There will never be any real quality management within an organization until the essential role of the customer is accepted and the practices connected to this acceptance adopted and implemented. The attraction and service of the customer is the second bottom line that a nonprofit organization must realize to be successful. If there are no subscribers to the programs or services offered by the organization, there is no purpose for its existence.

The quantitative aspects of an organization's customer base will be the purview of this section. Customer service practices will be dealt with later. There are three ways that an organization can assess its success in terms of the number of customers it serves, all involving scanning the external environment and collecting and maintaining current and comparative data.

It is incumbent on the organization's leadership to constantly scan the external environment to stay abreast of any demographic changes in the service area that may impact the organization's customer base, positively or negatively At the same time, an assessment of the current customers' needs may provide insights into any changes in the need/demand for the services currently offered. Such an assessment may also suggest some new customer needs that are mission consistent.

The third environmental scanning should involve benchmarking activities. The data emerging from the benchmarking activities provide at least a "snapshot" view of what the competition in the service area may be experiencing compared to the organization doing the benchmarking.

Based on the data from such analyses, strategic decisions can be made to address areas related to program development, customer support and recruitment.

It is recommended that an organization committed to quality management develop and maintain current and accurate data bases of its customers for at least three years. Such data bases make the processes outlined above simple for both the organization and the customer. The data can be segmented by specific program; service usage, and interest. The data can also be combined for total customer base purposes and manipulated longitudinally for comparative analyses and to determine trends.

In a later chapter the specific types of analyses and their interpretation and impact on policy will be developed. Suffice it here to say that since the organization only exists in the public interest, that public's interest must be the guide for the development and delivery of the organization's programs and services. Further, it must be this public's feedback that determines, not only the demand/need for programs and services, but also the quantity and quality of these.

The gathering of such data is the first step in ensuring an organization's commitment to quality management through the development and sustenance of programs and services for which there are demonstrated needs. The organization committed to quality performance will honestly face the results of these analyses and make the necessary organizational response based on them.

This is especially true when the data demonstrates a diminished customer support. Too many organizations and their leadership respond to these data with excuses or skepticism with regard to the data itself, rather than facing the reality that a particular service or program no longer has relevance, or that it is offered by other organizations in the service area, thereby creating a market glut.

The organization that uses the data collection methods described and that engages in honest assessment of and strategy formulation based on the results will be in the forefront of providing programs that meet current and future demand; thus, effectively ensuring the continuance of its customer base.

At the same time, these data provide a foundation for creating and initiating effective recruitment strategies and tactics to drive targeted marketing and advertising campaigns to sustain and grow programs and services; introducing the public to new or revised programs and services; and, directing appeals for philanthropic support.

The Organization's Return on Investment

The third aspect of a nonprofit's bottom line is the most quantitative and most resembles the for profit organization. It is the organization's actual financial position. This requires a multipronged analysis of the organization's current operating budget; its capital budget, if any; and the organization's total worth, including the value of its facilities and equipment, and also any restricted funds, such as endowments.

The assessment of the financial bottom line is the most objective. The facts are evident and should ideally be audited and reported by an objective third party. It is herein that the organization's leadership can best judge the success of the prior two aspects of the organization's bottom line: mission and customer base. Any resulting analysis of the organization's financial bottom line will clearly indicate whether the return on the human and financial investments is worth the efforts expended.

Most relevant to the discussion and analysis is the organization's operating budget. Its regular review provides an accurate picture of the organization's success and progress, as well as, the actual budget performance compared to the projection. The formulation of the operational budget therefore requires careful planning in its development.

It is important to attempt to develop a budget that is as realistic as possible. It should neither be an overstatement nor an underestimate. Use of some of the data reviewed earlier can be helpful in providing a support for the assumptions upon which the budget is based and the projections made. The use of these data should be a requirement of the development process.

In order to develop as realistic an operating budget as possible, front line associates, those who actually develop and deliver the services or programs, should be asked to offer their forecasts for revenue and expenses for their respective areas of responsibility. There are two benefits to this process. First, these associates have the ability to forecast better than senior management. They have the direct experience; likely direct access to attendance/participation data; and, they know their fields and current and past trends within their respective fields. They are truly the experts, so to not ask them is depriving the process of true expertise and experience. Second, senior management will want their "buy in" and ultimate ownership of the budget for the areas these front line associates manage.

This will require the senior financial manager to provide some basic accounting and finance training to help the other associates understand the process and to develop the skills required to develop the details of the budget for the specific areas. This will require some additional time in the budget development process, but it ultimately will be well worth the time spent.

It is likely that the front line associates' initial projections may fall into either the overstatement or underestimate category. Rather than summarily dismissing the projections, senior management should engage the individual front line managers in sessions designed to flesh out the assumptions and data support behind the projections. It is the goal of these sessions to adopt numbers for the individual areas of responsibility that are realistic, can be supported by data, and that ultimately have the support of the front line manager. Without this engagement, the front line manager fails to have any sense of responsibility for her/his operating budget. If the numbers are created by senior management and the specific area's budget doesn't meet its expectations, the front line manager will maintain that the numbers were not her/his, but senior management's.

The point was made earlier about the place teams have in the management of a quality organization. This collaborative budget development process is an example of its practical application. Again, the process will take longer, but the end result will be a more realistic budget supported by all those who have an impact on its parts.

It is recommended the budget development process begin at least three months prior to the month that the budget has to be presented to the board for approval and adoption. Larger organizations may want to even begin as early as six months prior to the start of the new fiscal year. This timing renders the operating budget a forecast, at best.

Some methods that have been employed to develop the annual operating budget with mixed to poor results involve such practices as taking the current fiscal year's budget numbers and arbitrarily adding or subtracting a percentage to address either inflation or an amount needed to balance the budget. This technique is rarely successful because the resulting budget will have no bases in reality, but be nothing more than a manipulation of financial numbers.

For years a method that was recommended and used by nonprofits was "zero based budgeting". It assumed that each year was truly a new year and started its development from zero and that the budget's net total was also zero, meaning that the end result of all expenditures and revenues was zero – a balanced budget.

There are some weaknesses to this system as practitioners have discovered. First of all, there was no recognition of any trending data in the creation of the budget's assumptions. More importantly, there was little to motivate the staff to excel if the end result was zero, nothing. Even if all the budget's assumptions were realized, there was nothing left at the end. More than likely, some of the assumptions will not work. After all, a budget is essentially a reasonable projection of what *may* happen. With no room for error projected in a zero based budget, many budgets ended in a deficit position as reality had its way with the budget's projections.

It is recommended that the operating budget be developed with a contingency expense line to cover unforeseen expenditures or revenue shortfalls. This should be about 10 % of the total operating budget's forecasted revenues. It is further recommended that there be a modest operating surplus projected in the annual operating budget. This surplus can serve as a "safety net" against operating deficits if the budget's assumptions are not realized. It can also serve as a pool for staff bonuses and other rewards. Another use of any surplus is the creation of a pool for venture capital funding to support startup costs for new programs or services. The third use of a budget surplus can be capital investment in new or replacement equipment, and facility improvement. All such expenditures are done at the end of the fiscal year and are shown as expenses in the final audited budget statements, thus maintaining the organization's fiscal compliance required to maintain its nonprofit status.

Another area of an organization's financial position is non-earned revenue. This includes all revenues not directly generated by program or service fees. The annual drawdown from an organization's endowment funds, annual philanthropic giving, and grants are some common examples of this aspect of an organization's financial health.

Endowment funds are intended to sustain the organization's long term viability. Most organizations take an amount, usually about five percent of the total value of the funds, to underwrite the cost of the organization's annual operation.

Senior staff and the Board have the responsibility of overseeing the return on these funds. Often this responsibility is shared with a third party professional or firm that manages the portfolio and recommends an investment mix. This arrangement in no way minimizes the staff's and board members' responsibility to be good stewards of these funds. Quarterly review of the funds' performance is standard. Annually, as part of the budget development process, an amount that the organization will draw down for operations is determined. At the same time, based on past and current performance and projections of future markets, the investment mix for the following year is determined.

An organization's Board has fiduciary responsibility for the organization's ultimate success and financial health. In the exercise of this awesome responsibility sometimes a board will be overly conservative in terms of the investment mix of the endowment's portfolio and thereby miss opportunities for market driven growth. Prudent counsel should be sought regarding the best mix for the organization and such counsel should be followed.

Endowments are about an organization's long term future and most experts subscribe to the principle that over the long term a more liberal investment mix will benefit the organization, as opposed to a more conservative investment strategy being assumed in order to protect the portfolio's return in the short term.

There are also some unwritten rules concerning the invasion of an endowment's principal. In the extreme, these maintain that under no circumstance should an organization invade the endowment's principal. Such a rigid stance has actually had a deleterious effect on the quality and viability of some organizations. There may be circumstances that arise for which an infusion of funds from the endowment's principal can actually save the organization or at least resolve a critical short term financial need. These may involve opportunities for capital improvements, new program development, consulting services and or specialized temporary staff. They are one time withdrawals, the rationale for which clearly indicates a real return for the organization long term.

A rule of thumb that has been used successfully for such actions is that the amount withdrawn is recouped and returned to the endowment in two years following the withdrawal. Some boards have treated such withdrawals as loans to be paid back with favorable rates of interest and over a more extended period of time. Such repayments are carried as expenditures in the operating budgets for the fiscal years involved in the repayment schedules.

Fund raising results need to be assessed and goals established for the fiscal year. Again, the initial projection should emanate from the associate charged with institutional advancement. The projection should be developed in concert with both front line associates and senior management, and should reflect a true advancement for the organization. The projected amounts should be supported by a specific fund raising plan that describes the various tactics to be employed and the expected amount to be raised through each tactic.

Part of the annual assessment of fund raising activities and the results of the efforts exerted must carefully weigh the amount of money spent on the fund raising activities, including staff salaries and overhead expenses, to determine if the amount raised is a reasonable return on the investment.

Bottom Lines' Assessment

The health of a nonprofit organization is judged by how successfully it fulfills the triple bottom line: mission fulfillment, a viable and growing customer base; and fiscal soundness. These are obviously related and each contributes to the success of the other. The assessment of a nonprofit's success must involve an evaluation of all three, and it is recommended that this assessment be done formally and annually by senior management and the board.

Often the evaluation consists of an analysis of the operating budget only. While, practically speaking, this is the easiest assessment, the isolation of that budget's results, gives only a partial picture of the organization's accomplishments and the fulfillment of its triple bottom line.

The contextual assessment of mission, customer base, operating budget, endowment performance and fund raising outcomes provides a wider and more complete perspective. The analyses' data can then be used for the development of realistic future projections and form the bases for effective strategic planning and organizational transformation.

CHAPTER 3

Strategic Plan: Blueprint For Success

Successful organizations don't just happen; their success is planned. Organizations committed to continuous improvement and the consistent delivery of quality programs and services use strategic planning processes to ensure their ongoing success.

Strategic planning requires the support of the entire organization to realize its potential as a means of facilitating total quality. The following will describe means to accomplish this engagement and also methods to produce strategic plans that will move the organization forward in its quest for total quality.

Often the efforts exerted in the creation of an organization's strategic plan are devised to create a document. Once the document is produced it occupies space on people's book shelves or computer files, having little relevance to the organization's activities. As a result those who were involved in the document's development consider their participation a waste of time. The process described below will offer suggestions to avoid these situations.

A clarification of terms is in order:

> *Strategy* – a direction that describes a path the organization identifies as significant to its improvement and growth.
> *Goals* – specific targets that the organization sets to measure the progress toward the accomplishment of a strategy. These are most effective when their accomplishment is time lined.
> *Tactics* – specific actions that the organization will take in order to accomplish the established goals. These should be both time lined and have measurable standards to assess completion.

It is important at the outset to affirm that strategic planning is a *process* not an outcome. If strategic planning is to serve as the organization's guide to greater success and improved quality, its process orientation must be maintained and reinforced throughout the organization. This role often falls to senior management and the organization's board, and it is a responsibility that they should treat seriously.

Before the process gets formally underway, it is an excellent opportunity for the board and senior management to revisit the organization's mission and either reaffirm that it is still operative or make the necessary tweaks to it to address changing situations. The organization's strategic planning should all be done under the mission's "umbrella" concepts. The specifics of the plan that will emerge through its development process will further the mission's vision and therefore ensure the future success of the organization.

The Steering Committee

It is clearly the board's and senior management's responsibility to direct the strategic planning process, but if one of its outcomes is the engagement of staff and the publics served by the organization, then these populations need to be engaged from the outset. To this end, it is recommended that a strategic planning steering committee be created. A member of the staff and a member of the board should be named to serve as co-chairs of the committee. It is their responsibility to coordinate the efforts, keep the process on task and on time, and to report on the process' progress at regular intervals to the various constituencies.

The committee itself should be comprised of at least one representative from each constituency so that the committee's final composition resembles the makeup of the organization and the public it serves. Its size will vary depending on the size of the organization and the number of populations it serves. The committee should not exceed a dozen people, if at all possible. Ideally, seven to ten people, in addition to the co-chairpersons is a workable group and should afford enough breadth and depth for any organization.

One of the organization's Executive Secretaries or a Senior Administrative Assistant should be assigned to assist the steering committee with its work.

While it may add some time to the formulation of the committee, it is helpful to its credibility if the various constituencies name their own representatives. When this process is complete, if the co-chairpersons believe that there are constituencies not represented, they may appoint additional members from the underrepresented constituencies. If the nominated members represent a single way of thinking about the organization or an over representation of any of its parts, the co-chairs can again appoint members to balance the representation. Once the committee has full membership, its composition and role should be widely publicized to the various constituencies.

The organization's Chief Executive Officer and the Board Chairperson confirm the appointments and meet with the Steering Committee to thank the members, give the charge, and develop a time line for the process' completion. They do not serve as members of the committee but may be called upon during the process for clarification or to answer procedural questions.

The Steering Committee's specific responsibilities include:

- Developing the strategic planning process calendar.
- Coordinating and facilitating information gathering sessions and mechanisms.
- Maintaining summaries of information gathering sessions and mechanisms.
- Disseminating results of information gathering sessions and mechanisms.
- Reporting progress to the various constituencies on a regular basis.

- Recommending to senior management and the board, strategic drivers which are based on the data analysis of the various information gathering sessions.

The preliminary stage of the process has three goals: engagement of the various constituencies; a determination of the current status of the organization; and, a vision of where the organization would like to be in three to five years. The actual plan will provide the blueprint of how to take the organization from its current situation to its desired future.

The span of prediction, the speed with which technology advances, the pace of change in market performance, demographic shifts and changes in the populations' needs, suggest that to attempt to develop a strategic plan beyond a three to five year time span is to doom any chance of success to failure.

SWOT Analysis

The steering committee's responsibility to gather information can be assisted in several ways. The easiest in terms of simplicity of participation and committee interpretation is to conduct an organizational **SWOT** analysis. This method has been used successfully by businesses and other organizations with excellent results.

The analysis seeks to determine trends and consensus from the participants as to the organization's current *Strengths, Weaknesses,* and its current and/or future *Opportunities, Threats.* These four organizational assessments can be based on items within the organization or from things external to the organization. A combination of both the internal and external factors will render the most complete and accurate picture. The end result should indicate areas that need to be changed to minimize any negative impact. At the same time the assessment will identify areas for growth and development and might provide visionary insights to the organizations' future growth and success.

The **SWOT** analysis' findings will lay the ground work for the emergence of the four or five areas that will drive the organization's growth and success for the duration of the plan. The organization will attempt through the specifics of the strategies, goals and tactics it will develop in the strategic plan to "accentuate the positive; eliminate the negative", as the old song says.

The easiest method to collect the information is to design a simple instrument to solicit feedback. A template for such a document is contained in Appendix 1. A random sample of each population represented on the steering committee is invited to anonymously complete and return the form to a central collection address, usually the executive assistant or senior secretary who has been assigned to assist the steering committee.

The more personalized the invitation to participate in the process is, the more enthusiastic the response will be. It is recommended that mail merges be used to individualize the cover letter. A template can be found in Appendix 2. It is further recommended that the steering committee representatives for the various constituencies personally sign the letters for their constituents. Finally, these should be sent first class mail with self-addressed stamped return envelopes enclosed for convenient return.

Projects tend to extend to the time one has for their completion. Acknowledging this reality of life, it is recommended that the completed responses be returned within 10 days of the mailing. If any of the constituencies' response rate is extremely low (less than 20% of the sample); a post card reminder to the original invitees with a 5 day return deadline may help increase the sample. A more complex and time consuming method would be to run another random sampling that excludes those in the first sampling. This is an example of the use of data bases that were referred to earlier.

Focus Groups

While the majority of the responses will come from such a mailing, another method can be used in tandem: focus groups. These are most effective when the groups can be so organized to have representatives of the various constituencies.

The potential focus group participants are identified at the same time as the mailing sample is created. There should not be an overlap between the two groups. A personalized letter inviting their participation in the focus groups and the personalized signature of the steering committee member representing their constituency should render the best response. Several dates and times running the span Mon. – Thurs mornings, afternoons and evenings should be offered, thus allowing the greatest scheduling flexibility for the participants A response card indicating the various dates, times and places that the focus groups will be held is included with the invitation to participate. First and second choices are to be indicated. A simple telephone or e-mail confirmation is requested.

The same ten day response time is given to those invited to participate in the focus groups, after which a simple telephone or e-mail follow up is used to confirm the final participants for each session.

In order for colleges and universities to involve a reasonable number of students in the process, student only sessions might be scheduled with an acknowledgement that students' schedules are different from others, especially in terms of the times of the day when they are most likely willing and able to attend.

In organizations that have shift workers, such as hospitals, focus group sessions should be scheduled at times that are convenient to these workers.

Each focus group is facilitated by a member of the steering committee. Another steering committee member serves as the session's recorder.

Each focus group's participants are asked to offer comments regarding the organization's' Strengths, Weaknesses, Opportunities and Threats. These are placed on a flipchart by the session's recorder. At the conclusion of this open ended section of the session, responses to the overall analysis are solicited.

During the third and final section of each session the participants are asked to rank order the top two items in each of the SWOT segments. This can most easily be done by giving each participant two colored stickers as they enter. Assign a color to each of the two rankings and have the participants place the stickers next to the items listed on the flipchart corresponding to their ranking.

The item analyses and rankings from each session are used ultimately to develop a final report of the focus groups. The item analyses are reported separately but also combined with the SWOT mailing totals in the final report. The cumulative prioritization rankings are reported separately in the final report.

Summary Report

When all the mail responses have been sorted and the focus groups' summaries tallied, a summary of all the responses should be developed. This summary should be organized in two ways: total sample responses for both mailed and focus groups, and a reporting by constituent group. Each group's response rate should be indicated. (Ex. Board: 6 of 12, 50%) Summaries of the focus group's prioritization should also be included in the summary.

The summary is then published in a manner that will easily reach as many people as possible in the simplest way. Often this is through the organization's website. Participants should be told the projected end date and the method of reporting the results at the time of their initial invitation to participate for mail responders and at the end of each focus group. A simple post card or e-mail to all constituencies indicating that the results are available and where to find them is also appropriate.

The steering committee will meet once the data has been assembled, and through facilitated conversations, develop a consensus on the organization's three to five strategic directions for the next three to five years. These along with the supporting summary data are given to the Chief Executive Officer and Board Chairperson for approval and adoption.

It is recommended that these two officers meet in person with the steering committee to receive and discuss the committee's findings and recommendations. This session also provides an opportunity for the officers to thank the members of the steering committee for their service.

The strategic directions recommended by the steering committee are then presented to the full board for its approval and adoption. If there is a period of time between the end of the development process and the date the full board meets, it is suggested that the full board be polled via e-mail, so that there is not a delay between the consultation phases and the actual start of the next sections of the process.

Strategy Development

The identification and selection of the organization's strategies are critical steps in the strategic plan's development process. It is through the accomplishment of these three to five directions that the organization will realize growth and success.

At the same time the selection of these specific strategies establishes them as institutional priorities for the span of the strategic plan. This is significant because to achieve the desired end results for each of the selected strategies the organization must be fully committed to their success. The organization's leadership, associates and every system and structure must be fully aligned with the key strategies selected to drive the organization's quest for success and total quality.

This priority alignment is perhaps most difficult to fulfill when it comes to resource allocation. This is especially true in an organization with limited or already stretched resources. In order for this total organizational support and commitment to occur it is imperative that the strategies be disseminated widely and that they be reinforced consistently and often, both in word, and more importantly, in deed. Any deviation from the key strategies, especially in terms of resource allocation, can jeopardize the credibility of the process and ultimately threaten the strategies' successful accomplishment.

How the strategies are worded is important both to their ability to describe the desired end result and also to motivate others to act in behalf of their accomplishment. Several examples might be helpful:

- *Increase graduate student enrollment.*
- *Develop new wellness programs to attract senior citizens.*
- *Initiate a major endowment campaign for Classical Concert Series.*
- *Expand geographic service area through new satellite centers.*
- *Improve grant funding for cancer research.*

Each of the examples uses proactive language to describe the positive outcome desired: *Increase, Develop, Initiate, Expand, Improve.*

Each strategy identifies a specific area for growth: *Enrollment, Wellness Programs, Endowment Campaign,*

Geographic Service Area, and Grant Funding. These become the areas that will enjoy the priority for funding and other resources in order to support their accomplishment.

Each strategy is further specified in terms of target populations or structures: *Graduate Students, Senior Citizens, Classical Concert Series, Satellite Centers, and Cancer Research.* Again, this prioritization provides clear direction to the plan's efforts and forms the basis for the final assessment as to the plan's ultimate success.

Strategies should move the organization forward; enhance its current success or offer a path to a better future. Strategies should not describe current operational needs or systems. (Example: *Balance the Operating Budget; Restructure Associate Performance Appraisal System)*

Strategy development is an essential preamble to the next step in the process: Goal Setting.

Goal Setting

In order to achieve the desired outcome of the key strategies, each must have a set of goals which describe specific measurable targets to assess progress in realizing the strategy.

While all stakeholders have a part in the development of the organization's strategies through the SWOT analyses and focus groups, the goals are best developed by those in the organization charged specifically with responsibility for the areas of growth identified in the strategies.

For the examples cited above: *Enrollment Management, Program Directors, Institutional Advancement, Vice President for Administration, Grants Office* are the specific departments or individuals who may be responsible for the areas identified as key strategies.

It is they who must take the leadership role in setting goals, but there are other departments that will be impacted by the various strategies. There are also likely to be individuals who have particular expertise, knowledge or experience related to a specific strategy. They need to be engaged in the process of setting goals.

The leader's creation of a cross-functional team to set the goals will ensure not only a collegial process for their development but also support of key individuals and departments that will be helpful to accomplishing the strategy. Such a team also ensures a greater sense of ownership for both the strategy and the goals. Human beings tend to support what they believe they have had a part in creating.

The goals are developed to provide specific benchmarks by which to direct and measure the progress toward a strategy's fulfilment. The goals refine the broader strategy statement and provide a time line and quantitative measure of success.

The following are samples of the strategy examples cited above:

- *Increase graduate student enrollment by 15% each year for the next 3 years.*
- *Develop 2 new senior citizen programs each year for the next 3 years.*
- *Successfully complete a $ 2 million endowment campaign in the next 3 years.*
- *Open 2 new satellite centers over the next 3 years.*

- *Increase cancer research grant funding by 30% over the next 3 years.*

    The target date for completion should have a specific date (Ex. By August, 2016) rather than *over the next 3 years*, used in the examples. Again, it is advisable that the specifics of the goals be developed by the cross-functional team, and not just the office or person responsible for the specific area.

    There has been much discussion on the role of the "stretch" goal and its efficacy. There are those who believe that the stretch goal motivates the associates more. There are those who maintain that a goal that is unrealistic, based on the current situation, past data and projected realities, does little to motivate, but rather frustrates the associates responsible for the goal's realization.

    The quantifiable measurements and the time lines can be negotiated by members of the cross-functional team through the development process. Again, data should be the final determinant as to what is reasonable, and at the same time, what will provide the organization the greatest potential for realized growth, and motivate the associates to believe the goal's attainment is possible, and even possibly able to be exceeded.

Tactical Design & Integration

    The evolution from strategy to tactic is a growth in specificity. The tactics are the actual road map guiding the accomplishment of the various goals. The tactics will outline a sequence of steps that need to be taken in order for the goal to be reached. The tactics are very specific as to quantifiable measurements, observable outcomes, benchmark timelines and individual responsibility. The cumulative total of the tactics will describe the logical and chronological sequence that must be adhered to in order to accomplish the goal in a timely manner.

Even though there will be a specific person assigned the responsibility of each of the various tactics, the creation of the tactical steps is best done by the cross-functional team that has been created to ensure the successful realization of the goal. The benefit of such involvement in the creation of the tactical design is the value of better decisions being reached by utilizing the knowledge and experience of those most likely to have a "stake" in the outcome or to be impacted in some way by it. The ultimate and more significant benefit derives from the engagement of those most involved. The collegial process creates an ownership of not only the goal, but the various steps designed for its realization. The team approach yields another benefit: the institutionalization of the final outcome.

None of the organizational goals can be achieved by any one person, but one person needs to accept the responsibility of leading the joint effort in terms of coordination, communication, motivation, and assessment. The person from the team who has access to the most information or experience, support staff, and administrative responsibility for an area is the best to assign to each of the tactics.

The first step in tactical design is to assess where the organization is currently with regard to the various goals proposed. What exists now? What has been tried before? With what results?

After the analysis of the current situation, tactics need to be sequenced in reverse order, using the end date for accomplishment stated in the goal as the beginning of the process. Working in reverse order, various benchmark time periods are established. What needs to be done in each of these in order to enable the final result is then developed. This is best done in calendar quarters, although there may be some tactics that will take less time and others more time. The quarterly system guarantees that progress will be assessed at least every three months.

It is advisable for the person assigned to coordinate the tactical team to communicate with the parties responsible for tactics in an ongoing manner, without being intrusive or domineering.

All members of the tactical team are present for the quarterly assessment sessions. The tactics scheduled to be completed are assessed first. Have they been accomplished? To what level of success? If not, why not and when will they be accomplished? The team can offer suggestions on how to get the tactic completed, establish a new deadline for completion, and at the same time, adjust other tactics' deadlines, if the changes made impact the overall successful completion.

Once the tactical design has been developed and supported by the cross functional tactical integration team, the specifics are shared with other staff in the various departments involved in the tactics. Regular updates on progress are also shared widely.

One of the benefits of such sharing is the sense of the organization's movement toward the realization of the goals. The sharing creates an excitement within the organization and a sense of accomplishment. Such momentum generates a sense of success that is contagious.

Strategic Plan: A Living Document

Effective strategic planning is essentially an ongoing process. The results of the efforts to develop specific strategies, goals and the tactics should be collated in one document and widely disseminated both in hard copy and electronic versions. Quarterly updates should also be disseminated in the same manner and to the same audiences. This ensures that the efforts of so many are not relegated to "dust collectors", but rather serve witness to the engagement of so many within the organization and to the organization's vitality and vibrancy.

At the same time the document should not be so "cast in stone" that its rigid interpretation and adherence leads to missed opportunities that occur within the time span of the plan, or that it fails to account for changes in the internal or external environments that can impact the organization and the accomplishment of the stated goals.

The document is intended to serve as a record of desire and accomplishment not servitude and constriction. Its forward thrust is intended to motivate and inspire staff and the public served by the organization to join forces in creating an exciting future.

CHAPTER 4

Board & Staff:
A Partnership for Quality

All the structures, systems and processes described thus far require people committed to developing and sustaining an organization committed to quality. At every level, in every department, this commitment is the force that binds people together in the desire to fulfill the organization's noble mission and realize its potential to inspire the organization to be truly great, not just one that beats the competition.

The people who choose to be involved with nonprofit organizations are indeed a "special breed". They are attracted to the organization's noble purpose and are often altruistically motivated to serve rather than to be satisfied. They often see their involvement as a calling rather than a career. They join other likeminded individuals in a partnership of hope to realize the organization's goal of providing quality service to the population it serves.

The Organization's Board

At the helm of the nonprofit's leadership is the Board. Its members share the ultimate fiduciary responsibility for the organization. At the same time, it is critical that the individual members have an understanding of and commitment to the organization's mission, vision and core values. They should be individuals who in their professional and personal lives subscribe to the organization's noblest goals and to their sustenance and advancement.

In addition, the board sets the organization's quality standards and leads all efforts directed at their fulfillment. In the execution of this responsibility the board regularly assesses adherence to these standards.

Unlike membership on a for profit organization's board, board service for a nonprofit is voluntary. Many of the other functions and responsibilities of membership are the same.

The board's membership, procedures, processes and structures are contained within the organization's by-laws. This document also specifies expectations of membership and a conflict of interest policy. Every year of her/his service, a board member is required to sign a statement that there is no conflict of interest represented by her/his board membership.

It can be helpful for a board member to have had some involvement with an aspect of the organization prior to being named or elected to the board; however, this can sometimes create a limited vision of the organization. It can create a sense of advocacy for the particular aspect or program in which the board member was involved, rather than a more global perspective that is more helpful to the organization and appropriate for a board member.

There is admittedly debate as to the size of a board's membership. There are several factors to consider in addressing this issue for specific organizations. First, how large is the organization? How many departments, sites, or divisions does it have? Is it a national, regional or local organization? Answers to these questions will determine the number necessary to constitute a reasonable number. Ultimately, the board size should facilitate its ability to function and effectively communicate. The goal is to actively engage the total membership in leading the organization's growth and success, not just amassing impressive names for the board's roster.

The board's composition should provide a wealth of expertise from various professions: law, finance, corporate management, fund raising, marketing and human resources. In addition, professionals from the organization's area specialty (Ex, health, education, art etc.) should also be represented. It is also advisable to have board representation from significant stakeholders such as major donors, corporate sponsors, and partner organizations.

Organizations that have an active volunteer base would be well served to have this group also represented at the board level. This can prove to be a "two edged sword" situation if the volunteer representatives are not properly oriented to a total organization frame of reference.

Common wisdom has often stated that board membership is determined by those "who can give" and those "who can get". These two functions are important, but their singular focus precludes active involvement in the board's overall leadership role in the organization's quality performance.

Further, common wisdom has offered the following simple triple expectation for board membership: Board members are expected to give of their *Time, Talents & Treasure* in the service and betterment of the organization. These can be specified in the following minimum expectations of board membership:

EXPECTATIONS OF BOARD MEMBERSHIP:

Participation:

- Attendance at a *minimum* number of board meetings, usually between 60% to 75% of the scheduled meetings.
- Attendance at meetings of standing committees to which the board member is assigned. Since this can be facilitated electronically, attendance at all the meetings scheduled is not unreasonable.
- Participation in fund raising and promotional activities

Advisory:

- Share expertise/experience to promote the organization's enduring success.

Fund Raising:

- Make a personal annual gift according to one's means. There are organizations that set a specific amount for this gift, but this might be

a bit heavy handed and may lose potential board members. The annual solicitation of board members should never be done by the staff, but rather another board member.
- Encourage others to donate to the organization. For example, in addition to a personal gift, a board member might solicit a gift from her/his corporation.

Promotion:

- Advocate for the organization and its good works.
- Communicate the value and benefit of the organization to those with whom the board member associates professionally and personally.

New Board Member Orientation

The value of a new board member's formal orientation cannot be stressed enough. An orientation session with the board chairperson and the organization's chief executive officer is scheduled prior to the first board meeting the new board member will attend. A packet containing official documents and organizational information should be prepared and given to the board member before the orientation session.

In addition, procedures and protocols of the board's operations can be reviewed, the organization's mission, vision and core value statements discussed, and, the expectations of board membership can be reviewed at the session. It is especially helpful to review some of the issues being currently discussed by the board and issues that will come before the board for action in the near future.

If time permits, a tour of the organization's facilities/sites will help familiarize the board member with the physical plant(s) and some of the onsite staff. Ultimately, the goal of the session is to have the new board member as familiar and comfortable as possible with the organization and her/his role as a board member.

Board's Officers

The board's officers will provide the leadership for board operations and standards. It is also this group, often formed as an Executive Committee, who will handle minor matters that arise between the scheduled board meetings. For boards that only meet quarterly, this group often has a monthly meeting with the organization's Chief Executive Officer to be updated on budget performance and any other issues that would require board attention or input. The following is a list of the officers' responsibilities.

BOARD OFFICERS' RESPONSIBILITIES

Chairperson:

- Calls and chairs all Board meetings
- Chairs the Executive Committee

- Serves as an *ex officio* member of all board standing committees
- Meets regularly with the organization's Chief Executive Officer
- Represents the organization at public occasions
- Serves as the organization's official spokesperson.

Vice Chairperson:

- Replaces the Chairperson in her/his absence, or as delegated
- Chairs the Advancement Committee
- Serves as a member of the Executive Committee.

Treasurer:

- In concert with the Chief Executive Officer and Chief Finance Officer, prepares the annual budget and presents same to the Board for approval
- Meets regularly with the Chief Executive Officer and Chief Finance Officer regarding the operating budget's performance
- Meets regularly with the endowment portfolio manager regarding performance and to review recommendations for investment policy changes. Brings these recommendations to the full board for approval
- Chairs Finance/Investment Committee

- Serves as a member of the Executive Committee.

Secretary:

- Maintains and publishes minutes of all Board meetings
- Maintains the file for all Board correspondence, documents, and minutes of all board standing committee meetings
- Chairs the Program Committee
- Serves as a member of the Executive Committee.

Board Standing Committees

Each board member is assigned to a standing committee. It is advisable to poll the board members' interests to ensure assignments that will engage the individual board member and for which her/his talents and expertise will most benefit the organization. It is within these standing committees that the board will interact directly with the staff assigned the responsibility for the various areas. It is essential that the board member's role remain advisory to the staff and not direct the efforts of the department or its leadership.

While there may be other committees that are specific to the nature of individual organizations, most nonprofit organizations can benefit from the following standing board committees:

BOARD STANDING COMMITTEES

Executive:

- Hires and evaluates the Chief Executive Officer
- Prepares Board meeting agenda
- Monitors progress of organization's strategic plan and reports findings to the full board at regular intervals
- Recruits and orients new board members.

Advancement:

- In concert with the Chief Executive Officer and the Institutional Advancement staff, develops the annual fund raising plan and presents it to the full board for approval
- Evaluates the effectiveness of fund raising activities
- In concert with the Chief Executive Officer and the Institutional Advancement staff, develops and evaluates the annual marketing plan.

Financial/Investment:

- Reviews the proposed annual budget and makes appropriate changes, if necessary, in preparation for its presentation to the Board for approval
- Monitors the performance of the annual budget and makes appropriate/necessary recommendations to the full Board for any adjustments

- In concert with the Chief Executive Officer, Chief Finance Officer and any third party investment counsel, monitors the endowment portfolio's performance and makes appropriate/necessary recommendations to the full Board for any adjustments.

Program:

- In concert with the Chief Executive Officer, recommends new programs or services and discontinuance of same to the full Board
- In concert with the Chief Executive Officer, annually evaluates the quality and effectiveness of all programs or services
- Advises the program/service staff on the development of new programs and/or new/potential customers.

Essentially, the role of these standing committees is one of quality control, ensuring that the various organizational systems are advancing mission, demonstrating progress with regard to the specific goals of the strategic plan, and meeting the proposed tactical benchmarks for success identified in the plan.

Two Controversial Issues

Two areas that give rise to animated conversation among board members are: board member evaluation and term limits.

A key aspect of a quality organization is assessment. It is through an analysis of the assessment data that the organization can measure its success in achieving the established quality benchmarks. The board leads the quality standard setting process and reviews the assessment data for the standard. It is reasonable to assume therefore that their work as board members and the quality of their performance also be assessed in order to maintain an environment committed to *total* quality.

It is recommended that the method be self-assessment. This should satisfy those that are offended by the thought that their volunteer efforts are being evaluated, and at the same time, assist the board member in her/his performance. A sample assessment instrument is included as Appendix 3

The matter of term limits is not as simply resolved. In organizations in which they do not exist the discussion will have strong proponents on each side of the issue.

The benefits of term limits stem from the regular revitalization of the board that naturally occurs as a result of sequenced and planned turnover. New board members bring a fresh approach and new energy to the organization and to the board itself. Term limits also allow for an easy way to remove board members who have not met the minimum expectations of their board service.

The longer board members stay in place the easier it seems for those with long tenures to dominate the conversations and the issues. Often they desire to maintain the *status quo* rather than leading the organization forward or even exploring new options. The longer board members stay in place, the more likely it becomes a *career* rather than voluntary service. Their partnership with the organization can so easily evolve into domination and control.

Those who speak against term limits often point to the "brain drain" that will occur. This argument is perhaps the best reason for term limits, because it presumes that no one else has any valuable ideas other than those currently in place.

The following is a term limits policy that has worked for several organizations. It addresses the need for fresh ideas and also at the same time prevents any potential "brain drain". Board members are selected and appointed for a three year term, which can be renewed for an additional two three year terms. No member serves more than nine years, and in theory, every three years one third of the membership is comprised of new members.

For organizations with no policy of term limits, the system can be phased in over the first three years of the policy being in effect. Gradually over the first three years all current board members would be replaced. This can extend to six years, or even nine years for organizations with larger boards.

The board members for each year's rotation off the board are identified at the beginning of the process, again ensuring that board members with institutional history and specific expertise do not all leave at the same time.

The Board's Role in Total Quality

The board's role in developing and sustaining a total quality approach to the leadership and management of the organization is key to its achievement. It is the board's role to set the organization's quality standards, model them in its performance, and assess the organization's progress at fulfilling the standards set. In the performance of this responsibility the board relies totally on the organization's associates.

The foundation of a successful partnership between the board and the staff lies in each knowing and respecting each other's roles and responsibilities. This seems such an elementary statement that one may wonder why it has to be said at all. Regrettably, and with all good intentions, in most cases in which the separation of authority and responsibility is murky or ignored, the resulting confusion can be very harmful to the organization and can lead to needless acrimony between the board and staff.

The board's role has been clearly depicted as the ultimate authority and responsibility for the organization's success and the quality of its performance. The board sets the standard and monitors its achievement. It delegates the details of the organization's operations to the staff. This delegation vests the staff with both the responsibility and the authority to achieve the organization's desired outcomes, employing the goals and tactics of the strategic plan as guides.

The Chief Executive Officer

The organization's Chief Executive Officer is the board's staff representative. For her/him to lead effectively, the board must afford the position great latitude in decision making and tactical operations. There should be few decisions that she/he must take to the board for resolution. There is nothing that more easily undercuts the position as her/his need to take *operational* decisions to the board. This does not preclude the Chief Executive Officer seeking advice from the board chairperson or the board's executive committee for decisions that may have significant or substantial impact. It is often good practice for the Chief Executive Officer to seek a "sense of the board" before making decisions with major impact or consequence. This in no way confuses with whom the operational decision making prerogative lies.

At the outset, the board needs to make its expectations clear to the Chief Executive Officer regarding the level of quality performance it expects both of the position and the organization. Clear protocols for interaction between the board and Chief Executive Officer are essential foundations to a productive partnership.

Frequent, honest and open communication between the Chief Executive Office and the board, or at least, its chairperson, is essential to guaranteeing the ongoing health of the partnership. These regular communications should contain both "good" and "bad" news items. It is bad practice (and poor politics) to "sugar coat" information shared with the board. The goal of the sharing is to confirm the partnership role. Nothing erodes the trust upon which the partnership depends more than poor or selective communication. At the same time, nothing cements the relationship more than honest communication. There is nothing worse for a Chief Executive Officer's position than to have a board member learn something, especially something negative, about the organization from an "unofficial" source, more often than not, the "rumor mill"

It is often stated that position titles don't mean anything. Actually, they are symbols that readily depict to observers the reality of one's position and authority within an organization. The nonprofit world subscribes to the meaningless of titles theory as can be evidenced by the title given by to the head of the organization's operations. Some organizations refer to this position as the Executive Director, implying by the title that she/he is "first among equals." A growing number of nonprofits have begun to call the organization's head the President. The former implies that the position has operational responsibilities with limited authority, often limiting financial, program, and personnel matters. The latter clearly indicates the position's full operational responsibility and authority.

Unless the board wants to maintain all responsibility and authority to itself, a situation which is unreal in terms of its scope and practice, the staff position in which it vests its responsibility and authority should be titled President. This is the title commonly accepted in most quarters as the "head of the organization". It is implied by the title that she/he is the final word in all operational decisions and the President also strongly impacts board decisions, through her/his influence. Practically, it forestalls "end runs" around the position by staff or others who will play the board and organization head off one another in a needless, and often, frustrating political posturing moves that do little to further the work of the organization or its quality.

This is not to imply that there will be times that the board and the President will disagree concerning either party's action taken or position held. It is imperative that these occasions be treated with the utmost discretion and confidentiality. Such disagreements are not to become the fodder for staff or customers taking sides, and as a result, protracted battles seeking a "winner" rather than a collaborative solution to the issue at hand. Once the issue is resolved, both sides must subscribe publicly to the resolution with no "second guessing" or criticism of the other side. In short, it is the organization's well-being that should govern such conversations, not individual egos or vested interests.

For the remainder of the book the organization's head, chief executive officer, will be referred to as President.

Hiring the President

A board's most significant decision is the selection of the organization's President. The long term impact of the decision cannot be understated. Therefore, the selection process should not be treated lightly or done quickly or in a haphazard manner. It will take time to select the "right person", but, time well spent upfront in the process will have long term benefits for the organization.

To meet the organization's needs in term of a leader and to satisfy employment law, the criteria for candidates should be as specific as possible without being so restrictive as to limit the pool of viable candidates from which to choose. Each organization must review its current needs and the directions identified in the strategic plan, and based on these assessments, decide what qualifications the successful candidate should possess. The specifics will vary depending on the type and current condition of the organization. But some general areas that should be considered include formal educational credentials, length of successful experience, at what level and at what type of organization(s), plus any specific requirements or talents that are relevant to the field of interest or expertise that the organization represents.

At the outset of the process three decisions, other than criteria, should be resolved. The first involves geographical scope of the search (international, national, regional, local). This will determine the extent to which the vacancy will be advertised and at what expense. Secondly, the board must determine whether it will conduct the search itself or with the assistance of a consultant or executive search firm. The greatest benefit to the consultant or search firm model is that all of the more detailed and prosaic functions, that can be very time consuming for board members, are handled by the third party. The firm will usually do the prescreening of potential candidates and present only finalists who meet the advertised criteria for the board's consideration. Thirdly, who will serve as the board's screening committee? Will it be the Executive Committee or an *ad hoc* committee formulated for the sole purpose of serving as the screening committee?

There is no way any single set of guidelines could possibly address the various types of nonprofits or their specific nature and condition, but some general suggestions that will address most situations are offered by what follows and would be applicable to either the self-directed or consultative model search and hiring processes.

Employment law governs a good deal of the search and selection processes. If the board does not have a member versed in either the law or human resources, the staff member assigned with these responsibilities should be consulted as to how to compose the vacancy announcement and the criteria statement. Suffice it here to say that a board does not want to so limit its ability to attract viable candidates because certain criteria are *required*. This is most often encountered in the educational credentials and length and type of experience. If, for example, "a doctorate in higher education" is required, then the organization is bound to hire only someone with that credential. Or, if there is an "at least five to seven years' experience in a senior leadership position" requirement listed in the public criteria, then only someone who meets the exact requirement can be hired.

It is recommended that this issue be given some flexibility by using the term "preferred" or "strongly preferred" rather than "required" for criteria. This allows the board to consider candidates whose other experiences and/or credentials may far outweigh the specific and more restrictive criteria. Obviously, if for whatever reason, the board determines that any of its criteria are essential, then the "required" designation should be used.

To save time and some expense, board screening committees are using technological or electronic initial first interviews. These can be arranged as either conference calls or can be done via Skype. The benefit of this first session is to afford the screening committee access to a larger number of initial candidates in a convenient and efficient manner. The goal of this interview is to discover the two or three candidates that the board is most interested in pursuing further. These few finalists will be invited to the organization for in person visits and more in depth interviews.

Candidates should be informed at the time of setting up the prescreening interviews that it is a preliminary interview and only the finalists from the process will be invited for an in person, on site interview.

In advance of the prescreening interview, each candidate to be interviewed is sent a packet of relevant information. The packet includes, but is not limited to, a copy of the organization's mission, vision and core values statements, the strategic plan, the most recent auditor's report and a copy of the most recent operational budget. Promotional or marketing pieces can also be included.

It is important that all the candidates interviewed be treated in the same manner. This involves, not only the actual interview, but the other arrangements, such as lodging, meals etc. for those invited for an onsite interview.

In advance of the interviews the members of the screening committee should develop a set of general questions that it will pose to all the candidates and also some questions that will be specific to each candidate usually seeking clarification of something that was included in either the cover letter or resume. It is also good form to allow the candidates some time for their questions. The caliber and direction of their questions can give valuable insights into the candidates.

Because the President of an organization will have a wide spectrum of contacts, it is advisable that the onsite finalists meet board members, other than the screening committee, staff, volunteers, major donors and community leaders. The candidates should meet key individuals with whom they will interface if awarded the job. A member of the Screening Committee should accompany the candidate to the various sessions.

Some organizations have found it effective and efficient to invite people from the various constituencies to a formal presentation that the candidates prepare on a given topic. The formal presentation is followed with a Q & A session regarding the content of the presentation. This affords a wider screening than just the members of the screening committee. It also allows insights into public image and presentation skills.

When the onsite visits are complete, a simple evaluation sheet is sent to everyone who met the candidate. This asks for an assessment of each candidate's strengths, weakness and risks. It is recommended that this be designed as an open ended series of questions, rather than a Likert Scale ranking. The responses are returned to the Chairperson of the Screening Committee and are collated and summarized by respondent type. For ease of constituency type identification, the evaluation form can be printed on different colored paper for each constituency. The summary results are presented to the Screening Committee for consideration in its final decision making process. A template is contained in Appendix 4.

Another assessment form is created for the Screening Committee to assist in its final determination. Prior to this form's creation, the Screening Committee members arrive at a consensus ranking as to the significance of each of the stated criteria. The criteria are then weighted with a numeric factor with the highest ranking going to the most significant of the criteria. Each of the finalists is ranked for each of the criteria, awarding each of the numeric factors only once among the candidates. (Example: If previous experience is rated as most important and there are three finalists, the candidate with the most relevant experience is awarded a 1, with the other two being awarded a 2 & 3 respectively) There can be no ties for this exercise in order to produce an arithmetic "winner". The ranking for each criterion is then multiplied by its rank order factor. (Example: If experience is the highest of the criteria, it is ranked a 5, the top candidate in the example above would be awarded a total of 5 in that category. The other two candidates a 10 and a 15 respectively.) An average of the Screening Committee members' rankings is generated. The finalist with *the lowest total score* is the preferred candidate. A more detailed sample can be found in Appendix 5.

This exercise affords the Screening Committee its most objective means of ranking the candidates. The finalist that emerges from this ranking exercise most fulfills the stated criteria. The Committee then has to evaluate any risk factors in the candidate being offered the position. If the risk factors are so great that they outweigh the objective ranking, consideration is then given to the candidate in "second place".

At this point the summary of the comments of others who met the candidates is reviewed and assessed. How were the candidates evaluated by those who met the candidates either individually or in a group setting? How far afield is their response from the committee's assessment? What risks, if any, were identified?

It is likely that a set of questions will have surfaced as a result of the in person meetings and subsequent assessments. These questions should be posed to the candidates' references. The specific questions based on the face to face meeting will focus the reference check to specifics, thus forestalling the reference giving the "walks on water" speech.

The candidate who emerges at the end of the process, the one who most fits the organization's needs and advertised criteria, is presented to the board for full approval. The Executive Committee is delegated to work out contract details within parameters set by the full board.

To many this process will appear rather draconian and needlessly protracted, but the selection of the head of the organization will directly impact the organization's quality performance more than any other decision the board will make. A thorough and professional process for hiring will impress the candidates as to the seriousness with which the board treats the position and the quality of the organization and its leadership. Hopefully, if done well, and all things being equal, the process will not have to occur again for some time, so the amount of time and effort is indeed worth it and should not have to be done again for some time.

President: Champion of Organizational Quality

The nonprofit organization's President has a challenge unique to the nonprofit world. She/he must serve as both the organization's leader and head manager. Contemporary theorists have made distinctions between these functions and have maintained that the organization's head should be a leader, not a manager. This may be fine for large corporations and even the more complex nonprofits, but in the "trenches" of the real world nonprofits, it might be a luxury that cannot be sustained. A healthy balance between the two is needed.

The President sets the direction for the organization's development and delivery of quality products or services. She/he also sets the tone for an organizational culture that supports and sustains quality performance. Through her/his visionary statements about the desired outcomes articulated in the strategic plan and through the President's commitment to modeling behaviors that give substance to the vision, the organization's noblest aspirations are confirmed and rendered believable. The vision motivates staff, inspires confidence in donors, and engages stakeholder support. This visionary role is the most effective and profound form of leadership the President can offer.

Part of this visionary role is to consistently espouse the organization's commitment to quality. The quality vision must be accompanied by the specifics of what quality will "look like" and how it will be rewarded, otherwise quality is only a nice theory. The President must set clear and measurable benchmarks for quality and expectations for the level of performance required to achieve them.

Such a culture is nurtured and matures in an environment of trust and caring. Regular, honest communication between the President and the associates is essential to creating and maintaining such an environment. In addition, the President should model a caring posture for the associates. One of the means to best accomplish this is to be visible and accessible in the organization. The old management principle of MBWA – Management By Walking Around – still is the easiest way to create an environment of caring for both the facilities, and more especially, for the people. These "trips" should be formally scheduled appointments that are given a weekly priority. These ventures forth from the "ivory tower" of the office not only afford visibility for the President, but also provide opportunities to meet and chat with the associates in an informal manner and to see the operations first hand. These visits are especially productive if they are unannounced.

At the same time, the leadership role of the President requires the President to be attuned to the external environments that relate to the organization's field of specialty and the organization's competitors. She/he must be aware of changing demands and trends; the competition's offerings; avenues of additional or new support; and, opportunities for growth. In this role the President serves as a resource to the organization's associates, since often they are so involved in actually developing and delivering the products or services that they don't often get the opportunity to see the world beyond their "shop".

It has often been said that the President needs to be five years ahead of the organization's current situation for there to be a viable future for the organization. This is true to some extent, but the President also must be connected to today's reality as well. The President must be more than the "philosopher king". She/he must assume a working and workable balance between the leadership role and that of the manager.

One of the most effective ways to demonstrate this balance is for the President to develop a formal system for communicating with the associates and dealing with operational issues that arise. Part of this requires that there be a perceived openness on the part of the President. There is no way that portrays this more than the willingness to listen. At the same time, there needs to be a structured approach to this communication. A true "open door" is not practical in terms of a President's priorities and activities that require her/his time and attention. However, one of the blessings of today's technology is instant access through e-mail and some of the social media formats, thus establishing a *virtual open door*. However, this will only be as effective as the feedback it engenders. The President's e-mail address and other contact information should be spread widely. Daily she/he should create a space in the calendar to respond to the messages. This demonstrates a real sense of caring and truly an openness to the associates.

In addition, regular newsletters generated by the President foster associate engagement. There are few things that cannot be shared with the associates. Such honest and open sharing creates the associates as engaged partners. The newsletter provides a great opportunity to publicly commend associates who have done exceptional quality work in achieving her/his goals.

To assist the President in her/his management function, it is advisable that the President form a group of associates, likely comprised of her/his direct reports, who will serve as the organization's Leadership Team. It is through this group's regular meetings that the President seeks counsel on organizational issues and receives progress updates on goal accomplishment. One of the other more subtle purposes for the creation of such a team is to model the benefits of interdisciplinary team work.

To the extent possible, the Leadership Team's meetings should be issues oriented and not "show and tell" sessions. This substantive approach will generate a seriousness of purpose that will give the sessions value and render them productive in terms of their outcomes. It is recommended that the facilitator for the meetings be rotated among the members, other than the President. This allows the President to be free to truly listen and be involved in the conversations, rather than being concerned with the conduct of the meeting.

The facilitator collects agenda items from the membership prior to the session, sets the agenda, which is sent to the committee prior to the actual meeting, and keeps the meeting itself on time and on task. Unless assigned to a specific associate, the facilitator also takes and circulates the minutes for the session she/he facilitated.

The individual members of this Leadership Team are likely to be department heads and therefore influence other associates with whom they work. It is expected that they share the President's enthusiasm for the vision and profess its significance and value in word and deed with their associates. They are also expected to serve as strong proponents of the goals and tactics developed for their departments in the strategic plan.

The consistent quality messaging is not "brainwashing", but rather the sustenance of an organizational culture committed to quality performance and the generation of a community of people joined in partnership to achieve the organization's noblest aspirations.

CHAPTER 5

Creating & Sustaining a Culture of Quality

Systems Thinking and Organizational Development

Each organization has a culture unique to itself. It emerges from a set of values that influences behavior and a belief system that informs the organization's choices and actions. An organization's culture is not written down anywhere, but the astute observer can sense it by viewing what types of behavior are valued and rewarded. The culture just doesn't emerge; it has some history, and as a result is often entrenched within the organization and influences the day-to-day operations, as well as, long term behaviors. As a result it is often difficult to change.

Organizational cultures that support quality are marked by continuous improvement, innovation, team work, and a strong customer/client orientation.

A leader's challenge to change the existing culture to one that supports and sustains quality is aided by a systems approach to thinking about the organization and organizational development techniques to engage the associates in the process of cultural change.

One of the aspects of effective organizational leadership that enhances the organization's operations in its quest for performance excellence is systems thinking. It begins with the acknowledgement that an organization is essentially a series of subsystems that are all designed with a common end in mind: the development of a product or the delivery of a service.

A systems approach to an organization sees the end product or service to be the result of a process of inputs, transformations, outputs, and feedback. All associates that have expertise or experience related to a project or decision are invited to contribute to the input phase and to participate in designing and executing transformations (changes) to the current situation. Preset standards for the end result of the process (output) are established upfront in the process by the process participants. The output is measured against these metrics and end user assessments. The findings of this feedback then become new inputs to the system generating further transformations that may be initiated to develop a more quality output. Thus, the cycle of continuous improvement is institutionalized and a dynamic culture results.

In reality however, the subsystems often operate as separate "silos", independent of one another. At times unfortunately, these systems actually work at cross purposes to one another, thus creating inefficient and ineffective work or delivery processes. At the same time, expertise from the various systems is not freely shared. Competition for limited resources creates harsh divisions among the functional departments. Ultimately, the organization suffers and the desired quality outcomes cannot be realized.

Since organizations are in fact human beings, if left to their natural inclinations and self-protective instincts, the "silo" mentality will prevail. The sum total of the attitudes and behaviors that result from such a situation creates the culture of the organization. Such work environments are unpleasant to work in, at best. Often there is an adversarial relationship between associates and the organization's leadership and a combative stance among the associates themselves, as sides are taken and strongly defended on many issues. Work processes are impacted negatively and associate morale is often abysmal. Work outputs are anything but quality. Mediocrity reigns.

Systems thinking provides a solution to such dysfunctional organizational cultures. It calls for each department or individual involved in the process of developing products and/or delivering services to maintain a total organization frame of reference and an understanding of the total process, not just the individual pieces. Part of such thinking always assesses how any change in one area impacts the process outcomes and the other participants. The benefit of such a thinking mode and the corresponding communication that results is a positive collaborative effort marked by a common concern for the quality of the end product and ultimately the satisfaction of the end user, the customer.

To facilitate such a culture the organization's leadership has to espouse systems thinking as an organizational value, model behavior that supports and practices it, and reward those within the organization who use and support it.

The culture is supported structurally by arranging the organization as a series of interdependent cross-functional teams, rather than a more traditional line reporting flow chart. The goal in developing the teams is to have everyone who has a part to play in the process on the same team. This affords everyone a part in the total process: planning, execution, assessment and revision. Such an arrangement provides a collaborative approach to innovation and the establishment of common product or service goals and quality control. Everyone is provided the opportunity to participate from the conceptual phase, through the actual development and delivery stages, and the assessment phase of the end result. Competition in such an environment is not between departments but rather among the members of the team themselves to produce the best product or best service, always with a goal of beating the team's best last result. Such internal challenges arouse excitement and creativity among the team's members and create a shared ownership, pride in the end results and strong associate loyalty.

It is a truism of human nature that people tend to support what they believe they have had a part in creating. This is the productive "mantra" of a collaborative organizational culture. Members of the various teams want to be the best at what they do. The team members seek to constantly learn the latest and best practices of their respective fields in order to enhance the quality of the team's process and its outcome.

The same systems model can be utilized by the organization's leadership to change the organizational culture. This process is known as organizational development. It engages the organization's associates at all levels in contributing to an analysis of the organization's current state, similar to the SWOT analysis used in the planning cycle described in Chapter 3. Based on the findings of the analysis, certain items may be identified as needing change or improvement.

For the outcomes of the organizational development process to be accepted and supported, it is critical to engage those who would be most affected by the change in the process. Cross functional teams are then developed to address each of the identified issues with specific interventions designed to effect the desired change or improvement.

The interventions are implemented with specific time lines for progress assessment and reporting, as well as completion. Again, feedback gained through the assessment process is provided to the organization and course corrections are instituted as needed. The process is dynamic in nature and offers a sense of movement and momentum to the organization's associates.

Because the success of a systems model is dependent on a process, instant results are not part of the picture, and should not be anticipated. This fact needs to be reinforced by the organization's leadership. At the same time, regular progress reports will provide feedback to the associates. One cannot understate the importance of this communication as a motivational tool. Another tactic that can help sustain the motivation through the duration of the process is to reward associates and teams as they successfully accomplish various benchmark moments throughout the process.

The culture of an organization committed to this type of thinking and acting is one that not only performs with excellence in its constant commitment to quality, but also has highly motivated, creative and engaged associates.

Cross-Functional Teams

Central to the systems approach to organizational development are cross-functional teams. Their benefits to the organization's operation and quality results are many.

As noted above, team members tend to be more motivated than those who work alone. The sharing with fellow professionals across the organization's departments and structural levels generates the ownership, creativity and loyalty referred to above.

The teams however are only as effective as the quality and frequency of the communication among their members. Only through frank and open exchanges of ideas can the process yield positive outcomes. These exchanges should be properly facilitated with an aim to arrive at a team consensus.

Consensus is reached through an open process in which all the members believe and feel that they have had an opportunity to contribute to the conversation without prejudice or bias. It is important for the facilitator of the session to create a non-judgmental environment in which the conversations can take place.

Consensus is not reached by voting on the issue. Voting can actually hinder the collaborative approach and also the final "buy in" of all the team members because voting tends to create a sense of "winners" and "losers".

Rather the facilitator summarizes what she/he has heard the group sentiment to be. The summary often can be a compromise position to satisfy both sides of an issue, but the goal of consensus has nothing to do with people's egos, but a solution to the issue under consideration by the team.

Once the team has arrived at and affirmed its consensus, all the members promise internal and public support to the team's final result and act as if the team's solution is theirs. Nothing hinders the positive impact of the process more than team members who campaign publicly against the team's consensus once it has been reached.

Consensus is not capitulation, nor is it "group think". The best unscientific definition of consensus is "all the team members *can live with* the group's final result". Team members presenting and supporting contrary or minority opinions should be consistently urged to present supporting data to convince other members of the value of their position. However, at some reasonable point, the question must be resolved and conversation cease.

It should be apparent from what has been said about the organizational development process, and specifically, consensus gathering, that training in group dynamics and facilitation skills are paramount to the process' success. If it is impractical to offer such training to all associates (which is ideal), then a cadre of associates should receive the training and these form a pool from which the facilitators for the various sessions are chosen.

Teams play to win. This reality of human nature has great benefits for the organization's ability to perform with excellence and quality. The team members tend to have a greater sense of self-worth gained through the support of fellow associates in a common goal that has value. But, this "winning" concept has its downside, as well. The organization's environment can become very competitive, stressing more the individual team's goal or tactic rather than its place in the success of the overall organization or a specific organizational strategy.

For a team managed organization to work, the leadership must balance each teams' autonomy with a consistent reiteration of the organization's mission and the priorities and directions identified in the strategic plan. Operational teams need a sense of self-direction to perform to their optimal potential. The broad parameters of the mission and strategic plan provide reasonable limits to this self-direction. It is presumed that those involved in the specific operational team know their fields better than the organization's leadership and therefore are the "experts" and their findings and solutions should be accepted and implemented accordingly. Part of the process also requires the teams to assess their interventions and tactics at regular intervals, thus minimizing the risk of total failure or disaster. The system also allows for mistakes and course corrections.

Meddling and micromanaging leaders have no place is such an environment and can easily frustrate or negate its benefits. A leader's unwillingness to accept a team's consensus, or her/his interference in the process once set in motion by the team, can have catastrophic results for the organization and totally undermine the system and its potential for producing performance excellence and quality.

One of the skills enlightened leaders have to develop is patience. Things done by teams will take longer; there are few instant successes in the process, but there are benchmarks to note progress. The leader can help the process by setting reasonable timelines for development of the teams' initiatives or goals and requiring that the team establish benchmarks to measure and report on progress. Unless the leader's opinion or expertise is sought by the team, she/he allows the team to manage the process through to its completion.

The leader can seek periodic feedback through the process in the form of soliciting from the team what has been learned that can benefit the final outcome of its initiative or can be applied to other operational teams within the organization. Such leadership behavior cements the *partnership* between an organization's leadership and the associates.

It is evident from what has been said that in order for such a model to work and have positive impacts, the associates have to be empowered to do their work. Social scientists who have studied empowerment have concluded that due to the level of trust and respect afforded the empowered associates they tend to perform at a higher level of competence and quality than less empowered or controlled associates. Empowered associates take great pride in their work output.

Leadership must provide the associates with proper training and organizational resources for the empowerment to truly be effective. One such organizational support is new associate orientation. This program should be directed by the associate's team leader, with an assist from human resources personnel, where appropriate, usually with the more banal aspects of employment. Ie, handbook, forms, taxes, benefits and the like.

In addition to introducing the associate to the other members of the operational team to which she/he has been assigned, the team's mode of operation, goals, and current projects are discussed. The team leader is also expected to review the organization's mission, vision and core values statements and strategic plan with the new associate. At the initial session some short term employment goals should also be established.

Most of the orientation will and should occur on the associate's first day of employment but there should be several follow up sessions scheduled between the leader and new associate through the first calendar quarter of employment. These sessions can have specific agendas or be open ended and directed by the associate's specific needs. During these the progress on the goals set at the initial session are assessed.

The scheduled follow up sessions are probably more important than the first day's and should be approached by both parties as significant and given the corresponding priority. It is at these session's that the leader can determine the associate's readiness for empowerment and to what extent.

Empowered associates tend to be engaged in the organization. They feel a real sense of belonging and ownership. They are loyal to the organization, its mission and goals; and, they will devote themselves selflessly to their accomplishment. They infuse their work with passion.

Associate Performance Appraisal

To sustain such an intense system and to ensure the performance excellence upon which the system depends, an associate performance appraisal system is essential. The system should provide structured and regular opportunities for the leader and her/his associates to meet to assess progress. Unlike traditional employee evaluations, these sessions are aimed at cementing the *partner* relationship between the leader and the associate, rather than sessions between *the boss* and *the employee.* The performance appraisal system serves also as the formal basis of any reward system.

Motivational theorists differ on the role and efficacy of associate reward systems as motivational factors. Further, opinions are varied and inconclusive when it comes to what type of reward system best motivates.

However, there is more unanimity concerning the fact that monetary rewards, while appreciated in the short term, do not serve as effective *long term* motivators. The factors that are most often cited for their long term impact on associate motivation are those non-monetary factors such as appreciation, recognition, career enrichment, and advancement opportunities.

Theorists and practitioners alike are also fairly unanimous in encouraging leaders to relate any reward system to the performance appraisal system, provided it is tied to the organization's strategic plan; and, offers the associate and leader some *measurable* criteria by which to assess the associate's eligibility for a reward.

While most empowered and engaged associates will find their work in itself rewarding, most look also for some reward beyond this somewhat metaphysical manifestation. Each organization should have a system in place that ensures that productive associates are rewarded for the quality of their work. The specifics will be determined by such variables as workforce size, nature of the organization's primary business and tax status, micro and macroeconomic conditions.

What all organizations share in common is their desire to grow in terms of their quality. This commonality sets the stage for performance appraisal systems and their reward systems. Within such structures, associates' demonstrated results are measured and rewarded.

An effective system will have two equally compelling goals: to reward associates for past success and to encourage them to duplicate the behavior that created the success. The specifics of the systems will vary from sector to sector and organization to organization, but ideally all systems will address the following.

Specific Measurable Work Objectives

The associate's part in assisting the organization to achieve its growth goal(s), as set forth in the strategic plan for a specific time period, forms the core of an effective performance appraisal system and drives the organization's success and quality output. These are arrived at though a negotiated process between the leader and the associate. Once the specifics are accepted by both, they form the basis of a *contract.*

The strength of this contract rests with the specific nature of the task(s); the time in which it (they) are to be accomplished; at what quality level; and, to what quantitative extent. All four of these aspects are to be included in each of the agreed upon work objectives.

It is the quantitative factor that forms the ultimate basis for the measurability of the associate's work.

Without this component, subjective judgment and arbitrariness govern the system and its interpretation, resulting often in frustration which mitigates against the motivational intent of the performance appraisal and reward systems.

There is considerable debate in the field concerning "stretch" goals and objectives. Those in favor cite the impact these can have on the organization's overall success. While at the same time, the opponents observe that these stretch objectives can have a negative effect on associate motivation and actually generate frustration and discontent among the associates. Care must be given to create objectives and goals that will provide opportunities for creative challenge, and at the same time, be within reasonable grasp of accomplishment.

In the final analysis, it is the *measurable performance* that needs to be assessed and rewarded.

Clearly Established Expectations

For a reward system to be credible, its parameters have to be established clearly and shared openly by the organization and understood by the associates. Such expectation setting provides an open environment in which to operate and prevents individual interpretation and inconsistent application of the system.

Since a reward system is predicated on the organization's and associate's demonstrated success, it is upon these standards that the reward system is built. It seems logical that three levels of expectation emerge from this perspective.

The first relates to the associate who has not met her/his agreed upon objectives in a timely manner or to the quantitative or qualitative level set in the established work objective. This situation presents the leader with an excellent coaching situation. The appraisal session's outcome should include clear indications as to why the objective was not met and what needs to be done to correct the situation. Specific corrective interventions are agreed upon between the leader and the associate and a recast timetable is established for the objective's accomplishment. If there are behavioral changes that the associate needs to address in order for the objective to be met, this is the opportunity to identify them and strategize for their development. Obviously, this associate is not given any reward. On the contrary, she/he is warned that repeated failure to meet objectives or change behavior can have serious consequences. Details concerning such situations are developed in detail in a later section: *Associate Discipline.*

The second scenario deals with the associate who just meets the objective. She/he is to be commended verbally, and in writing with a letter to her/his personnel file. Such associates should also receive public recognition in appropriate settings, such as, monthly newsletters and/or quarterly associate meetings. There is no financial reward given, but an assurance is given that if the other objectives are met in similar manner, she/he can expect continued employment. If the objectives can be exceeded there is the real possibility for salary treatment.

The third situation is for the associate who exceeds her/his objective(s). Commendation similar to that given in the second scenario described above is called for in this situation, as well. However, this situation has yielded results "above and beyond" minimal expectations. A reward has been earned and is merited, and likely to be expected. Salary treatment in the form of a financial bonus is appropriate. The associate should also be assured that continued performance at this level will also be recognized in end-of-year salary treatment and the possibility for advancement.

The scenarios have been developed for individual appraisal, but quality organizations are structured around a series of cross functional teams. The same system applies to their work objective development and assessment. One difference stems from the objective(s) and their qualitative and quantitative criteria being created by a consensual process.

Another aspect differentiates team assessment from individual assessment. Each member of the team is assessed by all the other members as to the level and quality of her/his part in the team's accomplishment of the objective. This can be quantified by a ranking system, the average of which for each team member describes the level and quality of participation and contribution to the overall team effort. This numerical assessment impacts the amount of reward each person receives.

All associates can expect in such a system to earn rewards for their excellence based on both individual and team performance. These scenarios are the **only** assessments upon which the performance appraisal system is based and upon which associate rewards are earned.

The performance appraisal system should have a direct correlation to excellence in associate performance and organizational quality. The system described herein creates an earning rather than an entitlement mentality among the associates and a culture in which performance excellence and quality work outputs are expected, valued and rewarded.

To ensure its credibility the system must be universally applied. It is only by so doing that it can be a motivating force for all associates. Organizations that have implemented such a system have high praise for its impact on associate morale and the quality and quantity of resulting work outputs.

Timely Response

Since the associate's objectives are time lined, the assessment of their accomplishment should be done as soon after the target date for accomplishment has passed. A simple electronic "tickler" in the leader's calendar can facilitate this.

There are three benefits to this format. First, it gives the leader several opportunities throughout the year to formally discuss the associate's objectives. Second, it eliminates "surprises" in terms of unfulfilled outcomes that may arise at traditional end-of-year evaluations. The more timely response allows for any corrective interventions to be initiated in sufficient time for them to have realized benefit to the organization. It also offers the opportunity to recast or reset an objective, thereby, guaranteeing its greater possibility for success. Third, if the objective has been met, the positive feedback and any earned reward that serve as motivating factors for continued productive work is given when it is most appreciated: when the job is done.

Meaningful Rewards

For a reward to have meaning, it has to be seen as something that has been earned or merited, not an entitlement shared with others equally. Therefore, one is led to question the real benefit of COLA and other "across the board" salary treatments. In reality, these can be disincentives to the more productive associates, since they are treated equally as those whose performance may be minimal, or even, substandard. At the same time, such universal treatments fail to provide incentive to the less productive to improve their behavior.

Even though earlier it was stated that financial compensation rewards do not produce long term motivation, it is a commonly accepted, and expected, form of reward. The more that it is tied directly to the accomplishment of the associate's objective(s), and proportionately to the organization's success, the associate will appreciate the financial consideration she/he is awarded and it may serve as a motivator for sustained positive contribution.

Often the nonprofit organization doesn't have a great deal of "disposable cash", unless such pools are planned in the budget cycle. One of the reasons financial rewards are limited to those associates/teams who exceed their stated objectives is to have a surplus above the budgeted amount for the objective(s). Part of this surplus can then be shared with the individual associate or members of the team responsible for the success.

Monetary rewards are always given in the form of one time bonuses, not as increases to base pay. Base pay is increased only if an associate's position responsibilities are increased or the associate is promoted.

Often the bonuses will have undesirable tax consequences for the associate. A flexible "cafeteria" plan approach to financial rewards allows the associate to direct the amount of the bonus to a preselected menu of benefit options with less tax consequences, such as IRA contribution.

Some organizations have also discovered that the associates really appreciate additional paid leave time as their bonuses. Other organizations award gift certificates to restaurants, hotels, sporting and cultural events to their meritorious associates. The means to acknowledge valued associates for the contributions they make to the quality of the organization are limitless.

Successful organizations take themselves and their associates seriously. These organizations have learned that there is no success without committed and motivated associates. It is this group of people who creates the conditions for the organization's success. That success is shared with them through regular and generous forms of rewards.

Another characteristic that these organizations share is their reward systems are based solely on **merit**. In such organizations associates are rewarded for their accomplishments, not their seniority, and only those who accomplish are rewarded. This meritocratic culture is recognized for its creativity, healthy competition, loyal and motivated associates: the keys to quality.

Associate Discipline

Because organizations are comprised of human beings, occasions will arise when an associate's behavior may require confrontation and corrective action. These occasions present great growth opportunities for the associate and should be approached as such.

All that follows presumes the behavior in question is neither criminal, nor identified by the organization as grounds for termination. In cases in which there are criminal infractions, law enforcement agencies will handle them, in conjunction with the organization's security and human resource officers.

In cases involving violation of company policy punishable by termination, the human resources department will advise the individual manager of the appropriate steps to take.

In both of the situations cited above, specific procedures will be outlined for the manager in the organization's associate handbook. The organization's human resource professionals will serve as ready support and reference and should be contacted at the earliest suspicion or evidence of criminal behavior or serious policy violation.

For all other behaviors the following is presented as a conceptual framework for associate discipline.

- The goal of associate discipline is always behavioral change
- Discuss the **behavior,** not the **person.** The behavior is observable and can be objectively discussed. Anything else will fall to subjective evaluation and thereby minimize the impact of the conversation. The more objectively the behavior can be discussed by the manager and associate, the less opportunity there will be for emotional, rather than, rational discussion and response.

The manager wants the person to commit to improvement, not feel condemned
- In the discussion of the aberrant or unsatisfactory behavior, some personal situations may be revealed. These should be treated with empathy or sympathy without the manager becoming overly involved in the associate's personal situation. Such situations must never be accepted as excuses for unsatisfactory behavior. If appropriate, professional assistance within or outside the organization should be recommended
- It is imperative that aberrant or unsatisfactory behavior and the contents of the disciplinary session between the manager and associate be treated with the utmost **confidentiality** by both parties
- For the best results, deal with the behavior in a timely manner, as soon as is practical, following the behavior's manifestation, or the discovery of unsatisfactory performance. Waiting until the next regularly scheduled performance appraisal renders the conversation "old news". Furthermore, valuable time may be lost to address the behavior and initiate behavioral changes.

The following steps can facilitate the above:

- Make sure that the facts are accurate
- Describe the results of the behavior on productivity and morale
- Converse with the associate, avoid preaching
- Establish the need to change behavior

- Create a sense of responsibility
- Gain mutual agreement on solution(s)
- Establish a timetable for improvement/changes
- Establish milestones to measure progress
- Identify a schedule for follow up sessions (progress report meetings)
- Describe consequences if progress is not made or milestones met
- Describe rewards for positive growth and milestone success.

The session's conclusions and other specifics are always committed to writing and sent to the associate for her/his concurrence. The associate is asked to sign and date all copies of the meeting's summary, agreeing that what is contained in the document is an accurate summary of the meeting and an accurate description of the terms and conditions of continued employment.

There should be only two copies: one that the associate signs and returns to the manager and the other that the associate retains for her/his files. At this juncture there is no need to make a permanent personnel file record. This ensures the required confidentiality and keeps the focus on a coach/associate relationship between the parties.

At the agreed upon intervals, progress is assessed and positive reinforcement given, if deserved, and help offered where there may not have been progress. Timetables and milestones may need to be adjusted to address the realities of the workplace and its priorities. While the strategies employed may be revised, the ultimate outcome of behavioral change is never sacrificed or abandoned. It is critical to the manager's credibility and the associate's growth and improvement that what is agreed to is maintained and followed.

A system such as has been described supports, and can actually enhance, the partnership between manager and associate in the task of accomplishing the organization's goals, while at the same time assisting associates to develop professionally and personally.

Ongoing Learning

Continuous improvement is one of the hallmarks of an organization committed to quality. There is no way that this can be demonstrated more, and have such a profound impact, as the commitment the organization makes to the continuous improvement of its associates. There are few organizational expenses that have such direct impact on an organization's success as programs aimed at associate improvement and development. Yet, it seems that dollars committed to such things as associate training are often the first to be cut during budget preparation or during a fiscal year when budget expectations are not met. If the associates are indeed an organization's greatest asset, then investment in this asset should enjoy a priority.

Ideally, each associate should have a three year improvement plan that is developed between the associate and her/his manager as part of the associate's performance appraisal. The plan should address skills that have been identified by either the associate or the manager as areas that could improve the associate's performance and provide opportunities for personal growth and professional advancement.

This type of developmental approach to associates requires the organization's leadership to subscribe to a belief that associates are more than functionaries who can be replaced, often at a cheaper rate of pay. Rather, associates' value is a paramount consideration in the assessment of the organization's success and any investment in their development and growth yields positive payback to the organization.

More often than not, the payback can have a direct impact on the quality of the organization's products or services and to the organization's financial success. These can be measured. But there are other non-quantifiable outcomes of associates' development programs. These can be found in the increased motivation that new skills can bring to the manner in which an associate performs her/his work. New skills tend to enhance a person's self-image, thus enhancing the positive energy the associate brings to her/his work. People engaged in development programs are not entrapped by boredom or "work ruts". All this positive energy translates into a culture of growth and a palpable commitment to the organization's quality.

Ideally, the menu of developmental opportunities is generated for a three year period corresponding to the length of the strategic plan. There are two ways to generate the selections: an associate needs assessment (Appendix 6) and specific skills that leadership determines are needed in order for the associates to accomplish specific aspects of the strategic plan's goals. A combination of these two will prove the most acceptable to the associates, and at the same time, meet organizational needs, as well.

Each year of the three, each associate, including the senior leadership, selects at least one of the institutional options and one of the needs assessment generated options. These are identified and committed to and serve as an aspect for review during the periodic performance appraisal sessions. The same procedure can be used tor operational teams.

While some negotiation between the manager and the associate or team regarding the options to be selected is appropriate, ideally and ultimately the process, to have its greatest outcomes, should be associate or team driven.

Sessions can be facilitated by either in house staff, human resource professionals, or external resources of which there are many who will do it *pro bono* or for expenses only. But an amount for the associate developmental program should be included in each year's budget and be awarded a priority to be spared from expense cutting.

In addition to these professional experiences, each associate should also be encouraged to engage in some form of personal growth initiative as well. These can include such things as weight loss, smoking cessation, exercise, and the development of a lifelong skill such as golf. While these cannot be as rigorously required as the professional skill development options, they should be encouraged and be totally associate directed. The benefit from these types of improvements may not, at first glance, be as obvious as the professional development activities, but there is compelling support from the medical and insurance fields that an organization whose associates are committed to individual wellness have less absenteeism due to illness and major health issues, resulting often in lower insurance rates. There are many agencies that provide in house free programs to address the various aspects of personal wellness. Group or corporate memberships can be negotiated with area fitness centers, if the organization does not have access to one its own. Memberships to these facilities can be used in the menu of rewards available to associates who have met or exceeded their work objectives.

The more the organization empowers its associates, the more it needs to offer opportunities for the associates to develop the competence and confidence to perform their work and achieve their individual work objectives. An organizational culture in which all the associates are engaged in their professional and personal development ensures the organization's consistent success and quality.

CHAPTER 6

The Customer: First, Foremost & Always

The characteristic that most identifies an organization's commitment to quality is its *absolute* dedication to the customer as the reason for the organization's existence. All the organization's structures and systems are devised and revised to afford the customer easy access to the organization's products, programs, and services. All the organization's associates are trained and motivated to not only meet the customer's expectations, but to exceed them. The customer's feedback is aggressively sought and utilized as an integral part of the organization's commitment to continuous improvement.

Significance of First Customer Contact

It seems so basic to state that outstanding customer service begins with knowing exactly who comprises the organization's customer base. Yet, some organizations make unfounded assumptions based on past history or uninformed hunches based on anecdotal impressions about this essential component of quality. Others subscribe to the "all things to all men" or "one size fits all" theories of customer base identification and eventual customer service. Neither of these approaches portend well for the organizations' attempts at total quality.

Unless the customer base is identified carefully and clearly, its expectations and needs cannot be determined. These must be known if the organization is to meet and exceed them: the hallmark criteria of quality.

There are several ways to gather data about the customer. The actual solicitations must have as their motivation the development of the best experience for the customer, and the facilitation of the organization's ability to delight the customer every time.

Some of the data can be gathered based on the initial point of contact and/or first purchase. This provides insight into the customer's interests, needs and buying trends. This first experience is the most important because first impressions are indeed lasting. In addition, the organization's goal is to develop the first time customer into a returning customer and eventually to develop a long term relationship with the person.

Nonprofit organizations have a distinct advantage over most for profits. There is, more often than not, a direct face-to-face contact with the nonprofit organization and its customers. The service is delivered directly and often immediately. While this provides great avenues of opportunity, there are also some challenges inherent in this personal interchange. Organizations committed to total quality will understand the significance of this initial contact and use it to full advantage.

How the customer perceives the physical environment of her/his first contact is very important in establishing a good first impression. Efforts must be made to create a welcoming, friendly, and accessible admission/entry area. It should be clean, uncluttered and dedicated to its prime purpose: greeting and serving customers. Often the entry area becomes a congregating point for the staff. A customer in such settings is made to feel as an interruption to the staff's conversation. Another "turnoff" for the customer is to have the entry area and its personnel engaged in projects other than reception, such as stuffing envelopes and sorting mail. Such activities often lead to clutter and again the customer almost feels that she/he has to apologize for being there, again as an interruption.

The significance and importance of the reception area and reception associates cannot be emphasized enough. Used effectively, the identification of the customer's need and/expectation can be worked into the initial greeting experience in a friendly and efficient manner. If a simple form is created, preferably in a computer file, several simple demographic and interest questions can serve both the organization and the customer very well for a long time. Care must be taken in this exchange that it doesn't appear to be intrusive and that it not take too much time.

The benefits of the time spent should be evident and rewarded. Often a membership card and number is given to the new customer at the end of the exchange or at least a temporary card until the more formal card can be printed and mailed to the customer. In addition to the membership card, printed information about the organization, its programs and services and ways of accessing the organization's website and other contact sources should be given to the customer.

Organizations that have multiple sites, programs and/or areas of interest, should make sure that the customer's interest(s) are identified and that the customer's information is transferred to the specific area(s) of interest.

In this age of instant and constant communication it is advisable to ask the new customer what the preferred method of contact is. Once this is identified, the organization should use no other form of contact. In addition, part of the materials new customers receive should have the organization's privacy policy that states clearly how, and by whom, the information gathered will be used, and with whom, if at all, it will be shared.

In order for this exchange to have positive long term results the purpose has to be seen as offering exceptional customer service, and as a result of the time spent at the initial contact, all future contacts will be streamlined, time saving and efficient. Customer service systems, electronic and other, should be developed to ensure that this is the case, thus rewarding the customer for the time spent during the first contact.

The process above assumed a face-to-face contact for the initial contact. All of the principles and practices also apply to telephone or computerized exchanges. These can be designed and orchestrated to be as pleasant and efficient so that the initial encounter again leaves a lasting positive impression of the organization. One of the simple ways to test this is to actually have a member of the staff pose as a new customer and assess such things as wait time, greeting, the cordiality and efficiency of the representative for the phone exchange. Again, a similar test can be employed for computerized systems, assessing them for their simplicity and efficiency. In all electronic systems, rapid turnaround of the requested material is paramount to impressing the customer with the organization's commitment to quality service. A benchmark of a one business day turnaround for the introductory packet to be mailed is recommended best practice.

Demographic data, once collected, need to be shared with appropriate staff in order for them to know who the customers are and to set about ensuring a delightful experience for them. And, while there are other ways the data will be used, its primary goal is quality customer service.

Some Cautionary Notes

In some nonprofit organizations the staff often believe it is their responsibility to challenge the customer's preferences by providing offerings other than those indicated in the customer preference data, in the hopes of "elevating" the customers' tastes. Such effetism only serves to irritate, and perhaps, even alienate the customer. Another variation on this theme is the staff choosing offerings based on their preferences, not the preferences indicated by the customer preference data. Such staff need to be reminded that their job is to meet and or exceed the customers' expectations, not theirs.

This is a particularly sensitive area when it comes to education. While it is clearly the right and responsibility of the teacher to have clearly stated expectations and learning outcomes, it may actually enhance the learning partnership and learning environment, to solicit expectations from the students at the beginning of the semester and to integrate these with the instructor's in the delivery of the course.

Another area in which the staff often neglects the customer's desires is the hours that facilities are open to the public or times that services or programs are offered. These hours are often made to serve the convenience of the staff and not the customer's schedule or preferences. Flexible scheduling for staff needs to be the norm, not the exception, in the nonprofit organization that is committed to fulfilling and exceeding its customers' expectations and needs.

Ongoing Customer Service Excellence

A great deal of time has been spent on the initial contact because it is so crucial in developing the long term relationship between the organization and the customer. However, there are ways to continually gather and measure customer input and satisfaction levels.

Periodic focus groups can prove to be time well spent for the staff, and at the same time, confirming experiences for the customer and the development of a long term relationship between the organization and the customer base. To gain the most from these sessions, they should be professionally facilitated, thus allowing the staff present to be in a listening posture. The sessions are not designed or intended to be platforms for the staff to pontificate or be defensive. It is critical that feedback from the focus group sessions is shared with the staff. Further, senior leadership can expect changes to be made based on the feedback.

Another invaluable source of customer feedback is the quality assurance surveys that are distributed to the attendees after each service or program. Again, the results can be computerized and gathered very easily. Summaries are generated and distributed to appropriate staff. How these instruments impact quality will be discussed in the next chapter.

Another way to gauge the organization's customer base and its needs and preferences is to conduct a formal needs assessment. It is recommended that this tactic be employed every five years and that its cumulative data be shared widely among board, staff and customer base. It is often very helpful to conduct this assessment in conjunction with the SWOT analysis in preparation for the organization's strategic plan development.

Significance of Front Line Associates

More often than not, a customer's approach and connection to the organization is made through a front line staff person. In a nonprofit organization committed to total quality, these associates are considered most important, and treated accordingly. Great care should be taken in hiring for these positions; they are more than "slots" to fill. Even more care needs to be expended in terms of professionally developing these associates and impressing upon them the significant roles they play in the organization.

Often these positions are deliberately maintained as part time for budgetary reasons and also to cover the many hours, days, evenings and weekends that most nonprofits have to cover. But, with creative and flexible scheduling the required number of hours can be served by full time associates. Such an expenditure will have long term positive "bottom line" returns for the organization.

Ongoing professional development is imperative in order to maintain front line associates' motivation and customer service skills. In addition, it is even more important that these associates be truly empowered to provide quality and immediate service. Essential to this empowerment is effective communication. These associates must know the organization; its services and offerings, and if they don't have direct knowledge they must be aware of how to obtain it easily and quickly. There is nothing more frustrating to a customer than someone at a service desk who responds to a question or a request with "I don't know".

The empowerment extends even more importantly to front line associates being able to make independent decisions to satisfy or exceed the customer's expectations. This includes making reasonable exceptions to procedures and policies in order to solve the customer's problem immediately and to her/his satisfaction. Another irritant to customers is the need for front line associates responding to a reasonable request that might be out of the ordinary with "I'll have to check with my supervisor".

Admittedly, such a staffing pattern will often cost more than is currently allocated for front line associates. However, if part of the professional development program involves upselling, cross selling and problem solving, there will undoubtedly be an increase in the number of long term customers and increased sales revenue. It also has been proven time and again that it costs more to attract a new customer than to retain a current one. Moreover, a dissatisfied customer will tell others about the dissatisfaction which will impact negatively on the organization's ability to attract new customers.

To this point, the practices outlined assumed a face to face interaction between the customer and a front line associate. All of the same practices apply to telephone contact. Special attention must be paid to wait time and electronic messages. These are the first point of contact for the telephone customer. Long wait times, irritating music, repeated "your call is important to us" messages all work against a quality customer experience. There is now a technology in place that generates a message that indicates the wait time and asks the customer if she/he would like a customer service professional to return the call to the number from which the customer is calling at the indicated wait time. The message also allows the customer to provide another telephone number, or to remain on hold.

In this digital age many people prefer to use some form of electronic access, be it E-mail or other form of computer generated communication. The same principles outlined above regarding easy access and quick response time govern the effective delivery of quality customer service and prompt and efficient response and solution to customer requests, complaints or problems. Where feasible, nonprofit organizations' websites should offer a live chat option. All electronic responses should always include the respondent's name, e-mail address and telephone number. Electronic responses should also include the customer's full name in the salutation. The use of first names, while intended to be personal and "folksy" is artificial, and in some cases, offensive.

Some complex nonprofits have created an ombudsman position. The function of this front line associate is to resolve customer difficulties and complaints immediately and beyond the customer's expectations. If an immediate resolution is not possible, there is an absolute guarantee that the issue will be resolved within 24 hours of the initial request. To be truly effective, the ombudsman's office should be covered for at least 10 to 12 hours per day, every day the organization is open to the public. It should also have its own e-mail address and have a prominent link on the organization's home page.

For organizations committed to total quality, the selection, professional development, compensation and reward systems for the front line associates are priorities. This prioritization will have financial benefits, and more importantly, the development and sustenance of long term loyal and "delighted" customers.

Complaints: A Source for Success

Organizations are human entities and therefore fallible. Mistakes will be made. Services and program offerings may be perceived as failing to meet the customer's expectations. These occasions can prove a treasure trove of feedback to ensure the organization's total quality.

For the exchange between the organization and the disappointed or dissatisfied customer to bear the potential positive impact on the organization and to retain the customer, several rules of thumb should be followed.

The adage that "the customer is always right" doesn't mean that literally, but rather that the customer is made to feel as if the organization believes she/he is "right" in the complaint. The first way to achieve this is to maintain a non-defensive attitude to the situation being described. If the customer has chosen to register the complaint, it is obviously how she/he perceives the situation in question, and that perception is the person's reality, so the organization needs to tread lightly. The best way to maintain such an attitudinal stance is to engage in active listening. Let the customer vent, that's why they have contacted the organization in the first place. If the venting doesn't provide enough information about the situation, a paraphrase of the substance should be offered in order to provide the complainant an opportunity to add more detail with less anger or frustration.

Once the situation has been accurately described and is understood by the organization's representative, an apology is offered on behalf of the organization, joined with a question to determine what the customer's expected resolution is. Any resolution that is reasonable should be offered on the spot. The more the resolution matches or exceeds the customer's expected solution, the more that customer is likely to be retained. This is one of the areas in which the empowerment of front line associates really pays off. There is nothing more frustrating to a dissatisfied customer than being passed up the "chain" to get a resolution of the situation.

If the person receiving and resolving the complaint is not an associate who has control over the situation that caused the complaint, permission should be secured from the complainant to share the situation in confidence and anonymously with the associate responsible for the area of concern. This provides necessary input for continuous improvement and also indicates that the customer's opinion is valued.

For quality control purposes, a record is maintained of all complaints received. A periodic review of this record can provide insight into what may be systemic issues that the organization needs to address. If a particular area or program seems to be the source of an unusually large number of complaints, the associates responsible for the particular area are expected to address the situation. In these ways the complaints are actually occasions for the organization's continuous improvement.

An attentive listener, an apology, and an immediate resolution, especially if it is the resolution suggested by the customer, will go a long way in retaining the customer for the long term. Dissatisfied customers will usually share their displeasure with others, thereby tainting he organization's reputation with other customers and/or potential customers. How much better it is to have the dissatisfied customer share her/his positive reaction to the complaint's resolution.

The skills to deal with such situations should be part of any ongoing professional development program for all associates, but especially front line associates.

Internal Customers

To this point the discussion has focused on an organization's external customers and their significance in determining an organization's total quality management. As important to the realization of the goal of total quality is an understanding of the significance of an organization's internal customers. An internal customer is any associate within the organization who has a systemic interdependent relationship with another associate in order to complete their common responsibility to deliver exceptional service to the organization's external customers.

Examples common to most nonprofit organizations are the interrelationship of information technology, accounts payable & receivable, marketing, institutional advancement and human resources and those who actually develop and deliver the services, products or programs, as well as, front line associates.

In an environment committed to total quality these associates treat each other with the same fervor and desire to exceed each other's' expectations as the organization's external customers. Each helps create the fabric of the organization's quality culture and total customer focus. To create and sustain this focus, information flow needs to be constant, data shared freely and widely, associates treated with due respect for their talents and expertise, and policy decisions made in a collaborative and consultative fashion, always reflecting on the impact these decisions have on the external customer.

Systems are designed, not for the convenience of the staff, but rather for that of the external customer. Policies and regulations allow for the flexibility needed to serve the customer's needs and expectations. The systems, policies and regulations are developed (and changed) as the customer's needs dictate. The free exchange of ideas in the creation of these between the front line and program associates and the administrative associates generates and sustains a customer friendly atmosphere.

Often with the best intentions, and the goal of efficiency, policies and regulations are developed that may not have quality customer service as their main objective. Often policies and regulations are designed to control associates' behavior in the development and delivery of programs and services, or to reduce the flexibility they have in addressing individual consumer requests or needs.

If in the development of the organization's policies and regulations, the various associate groups should treat each other as valued customers whose input is appreciated and needed for the overall success and quality of the organization. Such a collaborative effort will produce outcomes that are both efficient, effective and universally supported throughout the organization.

There is no tactic that is more important to the internal customer relationship than the sharing of information and data. Knowledge management is the quality organization's "secret weapon" for ultimate success. The organization's "information silos" must be dissolved and information and data need to be seen as essential tools for the efficient and effective management of the organization, and therefore, widely and often shared. Since most acknowledge that in the contemporary organization "knowledge is power", to share knowledge is to *empower* the associates: a key aspect of total quality.

If such an internal customer approach governs the interrelationships of the organization's associates, the collegial spirit that emerges will pervade the organization's culture, and in turn, motivated and enthusiastic associates will create and sustain the organization's success. Such a spirit is contagious and will have a positive impact on the organization's external customer base.

CHAPTER 7

Measurement: Quality's Assurance

James Champy in his seminal work, Reengineering Management (1995), states that "Numbers...metrics make statements of vision more substantive." His simple statement speaks volumes about the place and value of measurement as an essential part of any organization truly committed to total quality management. Unless an organization engages in regular and systematic measurement activities, total quality is mere theory and fancy rhetoric. It is in the measurement of *results* that an organization's mission and strategic plan meet reality, and in this meeting that quality takes root and is sustained.

Historical Context

The origins of measurement as a function of quality management grew out of the manufacturing sector's attempt to reduce the number of defects and substandard production outputs, thus reducing waste and ensuring a product that could consistently meet the customer's need and beat the competition. Organizations set production (quality) standards against which they measured actual performance. At various points in the production process, measurements were taken to ensure that the standard(s) set were being met. The various observation points' results were charted and summary data were compiled for management's analysis.

The goal of the measurements and their subsequent analyses was to identify points in the process where variances from the standards set occurred and the frequency with which these occured. Managers then used the findings to address the reasons for the variances, and by so addressing them, made changes in the process with the intention of improving the process output: a product that was more consistently "up to standard". It is worth noting that it was the process variances that were used as the basis for the process redesigns, thus giving rise to the "learn from your mistakes" mantra.

Another use of the data dealt with production goals in terms of the number of usable products that the process yielded. Production goals were set, always designed to improve upon past yields, thus setting the stage for increased profitability.

The various measurements and subsequent analyses eventually formed the basis of a very scientific approach, called *statistical process control*. Its proponents maintained that through careful and formal descriptive and interpretive statistical analyses, quality outputs could be controlled, and at the same time, the organization could engage in a process of continuous improvement, guaranteeing quality products and increased profitability.

The early iterations of statistical process control were seen as the exclusive purview of the production and engineering staffs. Later, and more contemporary, iterations speak to the *total* quality systems approach to continuous improvement, therefore engaging others in the process, such as marketing, sales, research & design, and finance. With these additions, other inputs have been added to the analysis process such as customer satisfaction data, consumer trend analysis, and competitive benchmarking.

These processes have been formalized today in such methods as: Six Sigma and ISO: 9000:2000.

Measurement in the Nonprofit

Admittedly, the historical use for metrics and statistical process control has been for the manufacturing sector. However, as the world's economy moves from a manufacturing base to a service orientation, it would be foolish to abandon some of the values inherent in the measurement and control processes that have proven so successful for the manufacturing sector for nearly a century. Indeed, it is a unique challenge for the nonprofit world to see the real value of such an approach to assuring the quality of it services, products, and programs.

As stated earlier, the total quality organization utilizes systems thinking and process management. Integral to these is the role of the feedback loop. The data gathered and analyzed through systematic assessment procedures provide a consistent and objective framework for the feedback. Moreover, if one examines the potential outcomes of a process that utilizes formal statistical analysis: better quality outputs, increased accountability, greater customer satisfaction, reduced waste, improved financial success, and organizational continuous improvement, to name the most significant, the efforts to adopt assessment tools would seem to be the proverbial "no brainer."

The initial challenge is an attitudinal one. Most nonprofits believe that their outputs and results cannot be measured, especially to reduce them to a number or statistic. This is especially true with educational and arts organizations. The furor generated by the nation's teacher unions surrounding the setting of standards for excellence and how an educator's performance will be measured against these standards, is one example of the resistance to measuring performance outcomes in the nonprofit world.

As has been stated several times before, one of the ways to reduce such resistance is to engage those who are to be measured in the development of the standards, assessment processes and corresponding evaluation/reward systems. Again, most people will support systems that they believe they have helped create. This is the recommended first step for all nonprofits as they begin their formal assessment processes.

As much as there are those who by nature and temperament resist any form of measurement, there are also those, who influenced by the same conditions, will want to measure everything. The organization needs to strike a reasonable balance between the needs and desires of its associates' left and right brain preferences. (A practical example of treating associates as internal customers, discussed in the previous chapter.)

The value of measurement activities stems from the assessment of an organization's results against a predetermined quantitative or qualitative standard. What is being measured therefore are actual results. These assessments provide actual performance based metrics upon which to judge an organization's quality. The data also serve as integral components of organizational continuous improvement activities. They can also be used as an objective component of associate or team performance appraisal.

Ultimately, the data accrued from systematic measurement activities offer the organization valuable information in its efforts to provide exceptional customer service and to sustain a culture committed to continuous improvement.

In addition to the measurement components of the organization's strategic plan and associate performance appraisal system already described in Chapters 3 & 5, the following are further examples of things that can be measured easily and impact the organization's quality:

- Attendance/participation
- Customer satisfaction
- Program outcomes

Attendance and Participation

One of the easiest aspects to measure is the number of customers who take advantage of an organization's offerings and services. Every program or service offered by an organization requires customers to gain access in some form, be it by prior reservation, phone or online order, or entry through a reception area. A simple head count for each day's attendees, such as museum visitors, or the number of tickets sold to a specific concert, for example, can provide valuable information to the organization in its quest for total quality.

In order for the analyses of the results to have value there have to be preset metrics established. These are best set by front line associates and leadership, rather than by senior management. Ideally, these metrics are created in a collaborative method, involving, for example, marketing and sales associates. Prior data can be used as benchmarks. Ideally, these metrics are established at the time that the next fiscal year's budget is being prepared.

Staying with the examples cited above, once the metrics are established and adopted as budget estimates, they form the bases for quality measurements. The museum then establishes daily, weekly, monthly and quarterly attendance projections. The actual attendance records for the various periods are then measured against the projected metrics. Often this is where the process ends; but, in the total quality organization, it is only the beginning.

The actual data is measured against the projected metrics and positive and negative variances from the projected metrics are recorded and analyzed. What circumstances internally or externally created the variance? These are documented and used in the development of future metrics.

By further example, if museum attendance spiked positively due to a special exhibit or presentation, perhaps more of these can be planned and the additional expense required to mount or develop them be justified by the assessment data supporting increased participation. If attendance exceeded projections each time there was a reduced entry fee for school groups, efforts to attract more school groups again can yield positive benefits.

Negative variances need also to receive the same analysis. These situations can often be out of the organization's control, such a weather. But, as often, some hard questions about the perceived quality or customer interest level may need to be addressed and corresponding decisions based on the analysis. In these cases, comparative data from the customer satisfaction surveys may add further depth and meaning to the attendance and participation analyses.

For organizations, such as museums, that have membership programs with various levels, usually based on giving amounts, the various levels can be measured, thus providing the organization valuable insights into how often the members at each level actually visit the museum and what programs or events they attend.

The number of new memberships sold by front line reception associates can also be tracked against a monthly goal that has been developed. If the goal is exceeded; some form of reward should be given, as described earlier. Any discussion related to the membership program should involve associates from the organization's advancement team.

Similar analyses can be performed by a symphony for attendance at its various concerts, season subscriptions, and music type preferences. Similar uses for the data gathered can help the symphony organization make decisions about things such as its offerings, marketing and sales initiatives, enhancement of subscriber benefit packages, and ticket price differentials. Again, associates from other areas who have expertise about marketing, sales, advancement and finance should be invited to collaborate on decisions based on the data analyses.

While attendance and participation data are the easiest to gather, it will likely also be the largest amount of data gathered for regular analysis. The data needs to be organized in such a manner that prevents the data from becoming overwhelming and therefore minimizing its value and utility. With the assistance of the organization's information technology associates, an IT consultant, or software package designed specifically to assist with attendance and participation analyses, the large amount of data can be managed for easy entry, retrieval and analysis. It is imperative that the program associates, who will use the data, are involved in the software development and/or purchase.

Attendance and participation statistics should be maintained for at least five years and appropriate comparative data year to year for the same periods or for the same events used to assess program and service appeal, utility and viability.

In addition to the internal uses for attendance and participation data, there are external uses that can have great benefit. Most applications for foundation and government grants require some form of self-reported data describing attendance and participation trends for the organization as a whole and for specific programs for which funding is being sought. The same is true for program sponsorship and major donor solicitation.

Such data is also a necessary part of any feasibility study for additional resources or capital investment.

Customer Satisfaction

If attendance and participation data are the easiest to collect and analyze, customer satisfaction is perhaps the most difficult because it requires the customer to invest time in responding to some form of data collection instrument and all the data gathered will be, of its nature, subjective. But, despite these two caveats, because of the prime role the customer plays in a high performing quality organization, consistent efforts must be created and maintained to collect and analyze customer satisfaction data.

Again, the starting point is the setting of a standard for a level of satisfaction that is acceptable or desired. This is best accomplished by discussions between front line associates and senior management that generate reasonable consensus. All customer interactions can be subject to this type of assessment, but realistically, those programs, events and services designed to attract the largest number of customers, or which have the largest investment of organizational resources, should enjoy a priority.

The preset standard is an average percentage figure at which, or above which, the customers will rate their level of satisfaction. For example, 92% or better of the respondents will rate the service, program, event as *satisfied* or *very satisfied*. The data from the respondents is then averaged and compared to the standard.

The design of the instrument from which the data is generated is critical to the credibility of the results. The simpler the design, the better chance there is for a good respondent return. The instrument should have two questions related to satisfaction: the Likert rating scale description of the level of satisfaction and an open ended response opportunity about the reason(s) for the customer's ranking. This is especially valuable and important for those whose rating was below the preset standard. It is recommended that a "forced" Likert scale be used to avoid the neutral option. A sample template can be found in Appendix 7.

Pollsters are divided as to the most effective manner for the distribution and collection of the surveys, assuming the instruments are designed to be completed by the customers actually filling out the forms and returning them. Retrieval is important for the statistical validity of the data. The method that has proven most effective for the organization in the past should be used. Ideally, if the majority of the completed forms can be retrieved at the conclusion of the actual event, there is no need for the customer to have to mail her/his response. The downside of such a collection method is the lack of reflection time.

Organizations have also developed simple electronic response forms for e-mail transmission and retrieval. A link for the satisfaction survey is created and imbedded in the text of the e-mail. For this method to be effective, there needs to be a careful coordination between the front line reception associates and/or box office personnel to provide accurate rosters of attendees. If this method is to be used, the survey instrument should be sent within two days of the attended event and an immediate response required.

The mailed option is the most expensive and the method that is likely to generate the smallest response. In light of these realities, it should be the option that is used only if the other two cannot be done.

Once the respondent data has been gathered and the averages calculated, the results are compared with the preset standard and correlations developed. In addition to the Likert scale results, the responses to the open ended question(s) should be summarized, especially the comments and suggestions of the respondents whose ratings were below the standard. It is from these that specific tactics may emerge to assist the staff in developing greater customer satisfaction in the future. Senior leadership should ask the front line associates responsible for the event being assessed for specific interventions that will be enacted as a result of the suggestions offered.

If the offering being assessed for customer satisfaction is one that is repeated with any regularity, the data are saved in order to do comparative data over a period of time, thus affording the organization an opportunity for longitudinal customer satisfaction data. These data can be used for long term planning and future program development. The data can also be used in the final determination as to an offering or service's discontinuance.

Longitudinal customer satisfaction data can also be used to track continuous improvement. If, for example, the 92% standard set in the earlier example is reached or exceeded for a period of time, the standard can be increased to reflect upward trending data. Unlike the negotiation between associates and leadership that generated the original standard, the new standard is based on actual customer response over a period of time. Again, a simple averaging of the responses over time can create a statistical mean percentage upon which the new standard is created. In an environment of continuous improvement, the new standard always exceeds the longitudinal average.

The use of the customer satisfaction data in conjunction with the attendance and participation data can provide valuable insights into the reason for an offering's level of customer interest and support.

Positive customer satisfaction data, especially longitudinal, can help make an impressive case to external funding agents, such as corporate sponsors and foundations. Positive customer satisfaction data, especially longitudinal data, can be used very effectively in marketing a particular event or program to the public and thereby impact new attendee/participant development.

It is recommended that, at least every three years, a more detailed customer satisfaction survey be developed and distributed to a random sample of the organization's membership or roster of regular attendees/participants or supporters. This is supplemental to the individual program/event satisfaction surveys. Its goal is to assess the satisfaction level of the organization's support and administrative services. Included in this assessment can be items related to advertising and marketing, customer service, pricing, facility cleanliness and overall perceived value of the organization and its offerings. Opportunities for open ended comments and suggestions for improvement should be included for each area being assessed.

The construction of these organizational surveys is more complex than the attendance and event customer satisfaction instruments. In order for the resulting data to have statistical validity and reliability it is recommended that someone in the organization with survey construction experience or expertise be utilized to develop the instrument. Another method of development is to contact a local college or university and have a student or a group of students in a research methods course design the instrument and also collect and interpret the data. The students reap the benefit of a real life experience and the organization gets the data it needs in a very inexpensive manner. One of the side benefits of this method is the instrument's design and data collection will be supervised by a professional, the course instructor. The one drawback to the student development option is that it may take a full semester to get the results. There are also consultants who specialize in polling, survey design and data interpretation. This obviously will be the most expensive method, but will yield professional results in a timely manner.

Once the instrument is designed, the bulk of it can be used repeatedly, or with minor tweaks, over a long period of time, and thereby affording the organization the opportunity for comparative longitudinal data.

Program Outcomes

The most challenging area to measure is how successfully the stated program outcomes were realized by those who participated in the program - the customers. The challenge stems from two sources: the outcomes themselves and the subjective nature of the responses.

There is indeed an art to developing program outcomes that will gather good data from the participants. Anyone who has struggled to develop learning outcomes for a course or program, can attest to the challenge first hand. First of all, not all programs require formally stated outcomes. There are some programs that by their nature and intent are pure entertainment. But, if the program or event has an educational nature, or any type of behavioral change as its stated purpose, then it can be measured against preset program goals.

Effective program goals clearly and succinctly describe the hoped for personal, professional and behavioral enhancements that a participant can expect at the conclusion of her/his participation in a specific program or event. The outcomes are described therefore in a positive proactive way with action words used to measure the specific outcome. What follows is an example of outcome statements designed for a professional development workshop on strategic leadership:

At the conclusion of the workshop the participants will be able:

- To appreciate the value of the **high performing organization** as an operating model.
- To understand the organizational impact of strategic leadership.
- To assess one's proficiency in the areas of strategic thinking, acting and influencing.
- To understand the role of a leader as a visionary and its organizational impact.
- To conduct a SWOT analysis of an organization or department.
- To integrate the SWOT analysis' findings with the development of a strategic plan.

A Likert rating scale is used to measure the extent to which each outcome was realized for each participant.

An average of the individual ratings is calculated for each outcome. These mean ratings are then compared to the preset standard, for example, a mean score of 4.20 out of 5.00 will be achieved for each outcome, using the traditional Likert ranking scale. If the standard is not met, discussions should ensue to analyze the reasons for the deficiency. Often the participants' responses to open ended questions can assist in this process.

Participants should be given an opportunity for open ended comment for each outcome statement. In addition, it is recommended that a few general open ended opportunities be offered, such as:

- *What aspect of the workshop did you most enjoy?*
- *What aspect of the workshop did you least enjoy?*
- *What suggestion(s) do you have to improve the workshop for future participants?*

While the program outcomes may be the most challenging to develop, they are the easiest to distribute and collect. The program facilitator or host distributes them at the end of the session and the participants are asked to complete the assessments prior to leaving. To guarantee some anonymity to the respondents, someone other than the facilitator of the program should collect the completed assessments.

A report listing the mean scores and open ended section summary is shared with the workshop's facilitator(s) and a copy is maintained in the office of the department sponsoring the program. Longitudinal and comparative data can be maintained for these data. Specific recommendations for improvement that are mentioned with some frequency should be utilized to enhance a program's effectiveness. Thus, the data is used for the continuous improvement of the offering.

Statistical Significance

Most of the statistical analysis discussed above would be considered descriptive statistics. Every effort should be made to render the data valid and reliable.

In the field of statistics validity means the extent to which data collection methods accurately measure what they are intended to measure and the extent to which the findings are really about what they profess to be about. The simpler the instrument used to collect the data, the more likely the results can be considered *statistically valid.* The more complex the instrument and the number of variables being measured within an instrument, the more the resulting data might suffer a lack of statistical validity.

Reliability in statistics is the extent to which data collection technique will yield consistent findings over time and also that there is transparency in how sense was made from the raw data.

There are some sophisticated statistical tests (t tests, chi square for example) to measure variable correlation and statistical significance between variables, but there would be few occasions when the test results would have any practical significant organizational benefit. Software systems such as Windows Excel have preset formulas for the calculation of these tests for any organization wishing to get more analytical statistical treatment of the data.

More importantly and relevant to the validity of the data is the size of the sample used to generate the data and the rate of return of the sample. Put simply, a sample is the size of any sub-group that is used to describe the larger population. For example, is there were 225 people who attended a concert, any data gathered from at least 45 (20%) of the concert attendees would render the data valid. Obviously, the larger the percentage of the population (225) the more valid the descriptive value of the data will be. All statistical reports should include an indication of the number of actual respondents and the percentage of the sample that it represents. This is shown as: *n=45 (20%)*

On some occasions the organization will want to create a random sample of a very large population, for example, an organization's membership list. While there are software programs to create these samples, a simpler and less expensive method is to run the membership mailing labels and select every third party in the list and use it as the sample. The same return rate expectations as described above would determine the data's validity and reliability.

After the time and energy expended on instrument design and distribution and the collection and interpretation of data, the presentation of the findings is important. Few enjoy or benefit from an extensive list of statistical data, no matter how impressive and valid it may be. The adage, "A picture is worth a thousand words" applies very much to statistical data. Every effort should be made to use the charts and diagrams that are readily available in the various software programs and support packages on the market today. Again, Windows Excel offers a wide variety of visual data display options. This formatting of the data will provide the widest visual appeal and broadest comprehension.

However, more important for most nonprofit organizations is the regularity with which the programs and services are measured, rather than sophisticated statistical analysis. It is even more important that the resulting data enjoy a wide sharing among the organization's associates and stakeholders.

Knowledge Management

The data gathered through the organization's assessment measurements and their consequent analyses are valuable assets for the organization and critical factors in its total quality management. Proper conservation and preservation of the data is essential to their long term value to the organization. Once a particular set of data and analyses are complete they should be stored in a central computer file, with a backup file of the data and analyses. The backup file should be kept in a location separate from the original file, and stored in a secure fire safe container. This preserves the data against computer corruption, theft, loss and destruction.

It is strongly recommended that there be an associate assigned to coordinate the organization's quality assessment activities, including data storage. She/he should be fairly computer literate and can have other responsibilities. For larger and more complex organizations the position can be full time and serve as the organization's Director of Institutional Research. It is further recommended that each of the organization's programs or service areas appoint a representative to serve on the organization's quality assessment team. The team's work is coordinated by the associate who has the organization wide responsibility for assessment or the Director of Institutional Research.

While the data and their analyses are to be maintained in a safe and secure environment, this is not to imply that access should be overly restrictive. The purpose and value of the data is directly related to the organization's total quality management. Therefore, a fairly liberal flow of data is an important facet of the process. Data saved and not shared are of little value or use. One of the initial functions of the quality assessment team referred to above is to develop organizational protocols for accessing and sharing data. These protocols govern the regular and extraordinary uses for the data and address access issues. The protocols are developed to support the organization's knowledge management activities and not to create a "secret, confidential" set of files whose benefit is lost or limited.

It must be obvious by this point in the discussion that there should be a degree of computer literacy required of all associates. Professional development sessions in Excel, survey construction, and basic statistical calculation and analysis will address this need. If instructors/facilitators are not available from within the organization, local colleges and universities can provide readily available and qualified resources.

A Closing Cautionary Note

Measurement is an essential component of total quality, but it can become an end unto itself, and thereby fail to achieve its goal of assisting the organization's continuous improvement efforts. Measurement is but a *tool* of quality performance, and for all its organizational value, it must be treated as such, and nothing more.

At the same time, credible results derived from the measurement techniques discussed herein will go a long way in establishing and supporting data based decision making within the organization, quantitative analyses as a basis for program development or dissolution, and ultimately, objective criteria for associate accountability and reward.

CHAPTER 8

Leadership: Transforming Theory to Reality

A nonprofit organization's journey to total quality is an ongoing process, one that requires the constant assessments and revisions associated with continuous improvement. The various aspects of the process have been outlined and discussed throughout the book. In most cases, the organization will have to engage in some transformational activity in order to adopt the various aspects of the high performing, quality organization. Successful organizational transformation doesn't just happen; it requires leaders whose skill sets complement their energy and commitment. These women and men translate quality theory into the reality of their organizations, their associates, and their customers.

For clarity purposes, an organization's leadership includes members of the board, the President, and the organization's Leadership Team. The awesome and daunting challenge of developing and sustaining a total quality culture within the organization and developing and consistently delivering quality services and offerings falls to these leaders. What follow are traits that leaders should possess in order to direct the organization's transformational initiatives and to render them credible and successful.

Visionary

A successful organization requires visionary leadership. The leaders must have a strong belief in and commitment to the organization's mission and translate these into a passion for the strategies and goals that drive the organization's success. The leaders' belief, commitment, and passion must be sensed by everyone within and external to the organization through the leaders' words, and concomitantly, through their actions. The congruent messaging that results imbeds the mission into the fabric of the organization's culture, and thus renders it operative through the associates' performance.

If the organization's mission addresses what the organization does and for whom, the organization's vision speaks to why the organization does what it does and what it is capable of accomplishing. The statement of an organization's vision provides the rationale for the organization's existence and the benefits the organization provides to its customers. It also provides a goal for improvement and growth. The vision is intended to motivate associates to consistently perform at quality levels because the need that the organization fulfills is important, perhaps essential, to its customers. The vision provides the reason the associates come to work each day, and why they find meaning and significance in the work they do. It provides opportunities for the associates to treat their positions more as callings, and not merely careers.

The vision also inspires those outside the organization to be motivated to support the organization and its good works through philanthropy, partnership, and patronage. One of the key responsibilities of an organization's leadership is to be the public messengers of the vision. They should aggressively seek out opportunities to share the organization's "good news". This is best done by enthusiastically sharing success stories that speak glowingly to the organization's positive impact on individuals and the community at large. While this effort can be supported by "talking points" developed by the organization's marketing professionals; it must be more than "spin", and obviously, it has to have a basis in reality and be something that the leaders present with conviction, eloquence, and enthusiasm.

While visions of their nature have some future "better place" aspect, they must also be grounded in today's reality. Current or recent successes give substance to a vision. It also creates a sense in others that the future envisioned can be within the organization's grasp; it can be achieved.

So many presentations asking for financial support are based on the organization's "need" rather than its vision. People are more likely to support a vision of greatness, rather than a message of doom. Therefore, the vision's articulation is an important part of the organization's fund raising activities.

The leaders' constant and consistent espousal of the vision will provide motivation to the associates in their efforts to advance the organization to new heights of total quality. At the same time, the leaders' efforts should not appear to be Pollyannaish. Leaders have to face the organization's current realities, but not wallow in them. Rather, in those hard times that all nonprofits face at one time or another, the vision should have the power to help people see beyond the present situation. By serving as a reminder of the significance of the organization, the associates can mount the efforts involved in moving the organization toward the fulfillment of the dreams espoused in the vision and the path to their realization laid out in the strategic plan.

Visions by their nature describe the dreams and hopes of an organization. Their expression needs to satisfy both the emotive and rational levels of the audience. There is a delicate balance that must be struck by the leaders in this regard in order for the vision to have its most positive effect. Each leader will have a style preference, emotive of rational, but as presenters of a message, she/he must learn to accommodate the preferred style with the other. Only in this way can the vision enjoy the positive impact of which it is capable. The most effective presentations will support the dreams and hopes with some current activity or longitudinal data that provide the sense of possibility that the dreams and hopes can be realized.

While running the risk of overstatement, organizations who want to realize their full potential; achieve their noble goals, and serve their customers with quality must have leadership that can ably and enthusiastically serve as visionaries. Only these organizations will have futures and excel at what they do and be leaders in their respective fields.

Strategic Thinking

As important as the ability to forge an exciting vision is for the organization, leaders of nonprofit organizations also need to be strategic thinkers. This skill allows the leaders to see the "big picture", and is thus related to the visionary skill. Strategic thinking manifests itself in the ability to set a strategic direction for the organization by identifying the organization's key drivers that will direct all continuous improvement activities, and by keeping the organization focused on them. Strategic thinking posits a clear direction for the organization that helps chart the course toward future growth and success. It provides a unifying direction from which all the organization's goals and tactics emerge and from which they derive their operational significance.

Strategic thinking facilitates the leaders' ability to abstract common trends from data, sometimes disparate, such as that gathered from a SWOT analysis, and to develop directions based on the analysis. This process is not to imply, in any way, that data gathered in a collegial manner is to be ignored, but rather simplified and focused for the organization's use.

At the same time, this skill is a necessary component of the leadership's ability to assess the external environment in terms of consumer trends, population demographics, the organization's competition and to interpret the "signs" of these as they relate to the organization's direction and continuous improvement efforts.

Through these functions the organization's leaders provide substance and specificity to the organization's vision. The leaders need to maintain their and the organization's focus on the strategic direction and the key strategic drivers chosen to accomplish it. This focus will, in turn, provide a real sense of meaning to the activities involved with the accomplishment of the associates' goals and tactics, and also foster a real appreciation of just how their efforts "fit" in the organization's overall future success.

Leaders need to regularly, and often, remind the organization's various external and internal constituencies what the strategic direction is and what progress is being made toward its accomplishment. These sharing opportunities should be designed to provide both good and bad news. In situations that the goals or tactics are not realizing the progress or success anticipated, it is imperative for the leaders to use the long term view of the strategic direction as a motivating tool. To have this stance yield its desired and credible results, the leadership has to have a certain objective distance from the everyday reality, without seeming not to care or be engaged. If the organization's leadership loses sight of the strategic direction and its intended outcomes, the organization is left with no one to "steer the ship" to its final destination.

Part of the skill development essential to effective strategic thinking is the leader's ability to navigate the balance between strategic thinker and her/his role as a member of the team. One of the ways this balance needs to be negotiated is the leader's avoidance of engaging in any political skirmishes, or "finger pointing" that might arise among the associates in response to a goal or tactic's failure to be achieved or perform to expectations. Leadership's role in these situations is to attempt a reasonable solution between the sides and to facilitate a collegially developed way forward by presenting the long term strategic direction as the unifying solution to the conflict. Going forward the strategic direction is used by the leader as the rallying point for conflict resolution and tactical redirection.

Obviously, the effective leaders do not take sides in the argument, but offer an objective analysis of both sides in order for there to be a constructive resolution reached by the conflicting parties. It is also incumbent upon the leadership to maintain an institutional perspective on those occasions in which the conflict is the purview of a discreet unit or department of the organization. At the same time, leaders must prevent any efforts to involve associates from other units or departments from joining the fray.

Put simply, the strategic thinking skill allows an organization's leadership to keep everyone's focus on the successful accomplishment of the organization's long term success and viability.

Change Agent

In an organization committed to total quality, change is a constant, driven by the intentional thrust of continuous improvement. In such environments there is little that stays exactly the same over time. The organization's response to customer assessment data; enhancements made in response to technological advances; and the development of new programs and services to meet changing needs and/or demographics, all contribute to the constancy of change's prevailing presence.

Few people are comfortable with change. Most prefer the comfort of things remaining the same. But, in the world of total quality with its demand for continuous improvement, today's success is but prologue to an even better future. It is imperative for nonprofit leaders to be aware of and sensitive to the organization's associates and stakeholders' natural tendency to resist change. At the same time, leaders have a responsibility to direct and support continuous improvement efforts. Again, this requires another of leadership's "balancing acts"

First, the leaders need to assess their own level of comfort with or resistance to change, and make the appropriate accommodations in order to place the organization's needs and directions ahead of their personal preferences. The value of the organization must always be given the priority. Herein is one of the practical applications of the strategic thinking skill referred to above. If the place that the change(s) has/have on the organization's long term success is stressed at the time of proposal and throughout the implementation process, some of the natural resistance to change might be lessened for the organization's leadership, associates and customers.

Organizational Development theorists have proposed a simple system to assist leaders in their efforts to gain support for change. It is based on systems theory of inputs, outputs and feedback, referred to earlier.

The initial step in the process involves an analysis of the current situation using available data from things such as results from the organization's assessment tools, best practice trend analysis, the organization's mission and strategic plan. It is highly recommended that leaders engage those in the conversation and analyses who are currently involved with the program, system or service to be changed, and those who may be impacted tangentially by the change. These people have practical experience and expertise that is valuable to the discussion, and it is they who ultimately will have to develop and implement the change. This is probably one of the most significant ways to demonstrate the real empowerment of associates.

In the consensus building phase of the organizational development process it is advisable to include those who have stated their objections to the proposed change, or whose history with the organization has been to fight any change. The logic of such a move is to, in a sense, "coopt the enemy". By engaging them in the process, their ability to later criticize the change from the organization's "sidelines" is diminished. Often this engagement develops them ultimately among the change's strongest supporters. They own what they have helped to create.

Once these analyses and conversations are completed, an intervention is proposed to address the consensus reached about how the program, service or system will be changed. Again, the more those who will be directly responsible for the change's run out are engaged in this step, the better the chances of the intervention's success. It is advisable to always allow a trial period for any proposed change. This has two benefits. It addresses some of the resistance or discomfort to the change, giving the proposed change a time to be tested, rather than "carving it in stone" from the outset. It also practically allows for those implementing and those who are involved in using the new service, program or system to provide feedback as to the change's value.

After the trial period is completed, a formal evaluation process ensues. The evaluation's feedback seeks to determine what is good and less desirable about the change, and suggestions for improvement. These are then assessed and revisions to the initial change are made accordingly. Feedback from end users is of great value in this process and should be sought aggressively.

The organizational development process as described will take some time, and indeed more time than a leader's mandating a particular change, but, the more amenable adoption and ultimate acceptance of the change is positively impacted by the process, and therefore, worth the time and energy spent.

The role of change initiator will often be thrust upon the organization's President. Often a board will either hire a new President with the specific mandate to make changes in the organization or charge an incumbent with bringing about organizational improvement through changes. The prudent President will certainly accept the board's challenge, but at the same time, warn the board that change usually brings with it some anxiety, and even anger among the staff, customers and donors. It is important that the board understands this reality and pledges support to the President as she/he begins to enact the mandated changes. It is also important to remind the board that effective change will not happen overnight, especially if the organizational development model described above is utilized. Finally, the board must also agree that if change is warranted, there can be no "sacred cows", particular programs that have assumed privileged status either through longevity, or an individual or group's patronage. If some services or programs are created as "untouchables", the credibility of the entire change process is jeopardized.

On rare occasions a change must be enacted without the consultative, collegial model being employed to enact the change. For these few instances, the leader's goal is not only to implement the policy or structural change, but to obtain support for the change. If the rationale for the change is logically presented and the leader's thought process to arrive at the change is clearly shared, often this is enough to quell most negative responses. These changes are, more often than not, mandated by changes in the law or are solutions to extreme organizational circumstances that require more immediate resolution than the consultative process allows for.

Education is one of the ways to assist associates and others involved with the organization to come to terms with changes that are about to be enacted, or those that have already been initiated. Ideally, if the educational activities can be offered prior to the change's implementation, it will increase the opportunity for greater acceptance. In its simplest form, sharing the background and rationale for the change is very helpful. If the change has been adopted elsewhere by similar organizations, sharing the benefits of the change for these organizations is also helpful. One of the reasons people tend to resist change is the fear that they may not have the skills or background to be able to adapt to the new requirements. Leadership's proactive stance in providing either in house or external skill development sessions will go a long way to lessening the fear.

It should be obvious from what has been developed thus far that unilateral, top-down sudden change will be disruptive to the organization, perhaps even long term. Most people are reasonable, if approached in a reasonable manner by the organization's leadership concerning the need for the change, they will accept and support the change. Ideally, time permitting, engaging those most to be effected by the change in the process of its development, will ensure a wider support and acceptance.

Continuous improvement which is the driving force for a quality organization's change provides opportunities for expressions of the leadership and associates' creativity. This organizational characteristic comes more naturally to some organizations, such as arts and education, but should be an aspect that the leadership models, and enthusiastically encourages and supports, in all nonprofit organizations. It is through the unbridled exercise of the many creative talents within an organization that the best ideas will emerge. Creative solutions mark successful organizations.

There are times that the leader will think or feel that it is easier to just leave things the way they are: the "don't fix if not broke" school of change. This attitude is dangerous and ultimately could have devastating effects on the organization that subscribes to this non-change position. A static organization can very easily evolve into a stale organization.

There are other times that the leader will just not have the patience for the process required to promote effective change or to tolerate the negative expressions that the natural resistance to change will engender. At these times, it is important for the leader to remember the long term benefits of the proposed change and to reflect that the organization that is changing is alive and dynamic.

Results Oriented

It is evident from all that has been said about total quality management that all its efforts are directed at leading the organization to greater levels of excellence and success. In addition to the leadership characteristics discussed above there must be a consistent dedication and attention to achieving results. The accomplishment of the strategic plan's goals, realizing or exceeding the attendance/participation targets set, meeting or beating budgetary projections are examples of results that determine the organization's quality output.

Concrete results are the measure of the organization's success and quality. Often good intentions are accepted as substitutes for goal attainment. It is not enough for associates to *try* they must *produce* measureable success.

It is the responsibility of the organization's leadership to foster a culture that values and rewards results. This requires leadership to set the tone for such a cultural transformation. A collegial approach to goal setting, associate empowerment, and a viable and credible associate reward system all support an organizational environment that gives results their essential place as determinants of accountability, excellence and success.

Leaders must provide challenge and support to the associates in their roles as the creators and deliverers of the organization's services and offerings. Challenge and support are the foundations of motivation.

Challenge has two aspects: proactive and reactive. It is critical that the organization's leadership knows when and how to use each. The former provides the initial "spark to light the creative fires" within the associates. It also encourages the associates to stretch beyond previous levels of success. Through its use, the challenge aspect also provides an entrepreneurial sense of ownership within the associate or team charged with creating something new or building on past successes.

Challenge also has a confrontational aspect that can serve as a midcourse correction to the development process or the determination of what went wrong if the results are not realized, and also what has been learned from the failure.

To be truly effective as a motivational tool, both of these aspects of challenge must demonstrate a real sense of *partnership* between the associate/team and the leader.

Support is shown by the leaders' manifestation of genuine caring, not only for the result, but also the associate/team involved in the development and implementation phases of a project. It calls for giving honest feedback. At times support will be shown by encouraging disenchanted or frustrated associates. This is often best accomplished, and appreciated, if it is demonstrated in a personal and an institutional manner. The leader's offer of her/his assistance and making resources available to assist the associates /team in their efforts will often go a long way to addressing the project's and associates' needs.

The supportive role is clearest in the leaders' acknowledgement and gratitude for the end result being achieved, or better, exceeded. Methods of rewards and their long term impact on associate behavior and organizational excellence have already been discussed earlier.

There is often an associate reaction to the leadership's insistence on results. It is expressed in different ways, but most often, in statements like "All she/he cares about is the numbers." This can be symptomatic of an over emphasis on the measureable results at the expense of the people performing the tasks. If care is taken to engage the associates in the development of the projected results, and if leadership regularly offers challenge and support through the process, this situation should not arise too often. Effective leadership manifests a balance between production and people and this equanimity is a learned skill, fine-tuned over time by the leaders' ability to read each situation's need and to respond with the motivational aspect with the greatest potential for success in terms of the desired result(s) and the associate(s).

Integrity

Nonprofit organizations exist for the *public interest.* Their services and offerings ennoble and enrich the lives of the publics they serve. In many ways, and correctly so, nonprofit organizations are held to a higher standard in the manner that they conduct their business. Nonprofit leaders must acknowledge and accept this august responsibility and act with integrity in all their dealings. At the same time, acting with integrity will shape the attitudes and behavior of the organization's associates and set a level of expectation for the organization's stakeholders and suppliers. To act with integrity means that public and private behavior is guided by honesty, fairness, and courage: an integrity of character; an integrity of relationship; and an integrity of action.

This begins with the leaders being true to themselves. Their actions must always be above reproach, both in public and in private. Their leadership positions are held in service to the public interest for which the organization was founded. Nonprofit leaders are very often the "face" of the organization and their behavior is evident. They are constantly at the mercy of public opinion, and these opinions will reflect back on the organization, positively or negatively. But more important than using what others may think of one's behavior as a measure of integrity, there is another more significant consideration.

All honesty begins with honesty of character. Polonius' sage advice to his son, Laertes in <u>Hamlet</u>, "To thine own self be true", is more relevant as a life principle for today's leaders, than it may have been in Shakespeare's times. This honesty stems from a clear understanding and acceptance of who the leaders are as persons, and what principles and values guide their behaviors. The consistency between the internal and external dimensions of this awareness provides the basis for living with integrity. It implies that a person in a leadership position will never act contrary to her/his own code of conduct and value system. This is the "stuff" of which heroes are made. It is hoped that nonprofit leaders will rarely be called upon to perform acts of heroism in the exercise of their responsibilities, but it is the ultimate test of integrity.

This standard of personal integrity can be demonstrated less dramatically in the daily performance of the leaders' service. An attitude and its corresponding behavior that flows from this principle impacts the interaction between the leader and the organization's associates when it comes to actions required of the associates. The leader who practices honesty of character will never ask an associate to do anything that the leader her/himself wouldn't do, or that is contrary to the associate's value system. Again, one assumes that occurrences of this kind would be rare.

This integrity of character governs the leaders' communication. Essentially, this manifests itself in telling the truth, regardless of the consequences of such honesty. So much of what has been offered as means to creating and sustaining an organization committed to total quality involves the leaders' ability to effectively communicate with the organization's many publics. Honesty is the foundation upon which these communication exchanges build trust and respect.

There is a temptation in today's communications to succumb to the practice of creating and delivering messages that offer "spin" rather than truth. Consistency of messaging in this environment has little to do with the truth of the message, but rather that the statements are "on message". Other practices that lessen the integrity of communication involve adapting the truth to fit the circumstance or audience, and "sugarcoating" information, especially bad news. In addition to the lack of integrity involved in these practices, they do no favors for the organization or its public support in the long term.

When an organization's leadership is recognized for its honesty, deep respect and trust are natural results and these positive feelings revert back to the organization and its mission.

Integrity demands that the nonprofit organization's leadership act on a higher level than the mere compliance to a law or code. Rather the leaders should celebrate the spirit of the law or code. In so doing, the leaders exhibit integrity of relationship.

When acting with an integrity of relationship leaders treat their professional colleagues and associates with respect, affording each of them the dignity of which they are deserving. In such an organization, interpersonal relationships are free of harassment, manipulation, condescension, prejudice, and discrimination. While there are laws that govern many of these behaviors, the leaders acting with an integrity of relationship will be more concerned about doing the *right* thing rather than what is *legal*. It might seem trite, but the Golden Rule of "do unto others as you would want others to do unto you" speaks eloquently and simply to the foundation of interpersonal relationships that are based on integrity.

Integrity of relationship inspires leaders to respect others in the organization for their talents and expertise and to offer opportunities to express them, thus generating a work environment for the associates that is personally and professionally fulfilling. In such an organizational culture, behavioral expectations are modeled rather than mandated.

Another important manifestation of integrity of relationship is the level of trust that leaders place in their associates. This trust is shown in a prevailing attitude set by the organization's leadership that believes that the associates will always do their best to promote and sustain the organization's mission, and that they will always do what is right and best in terms of the performance of their duties and the satisfaction of the customers. The investment of trust will have a great return in terms of loyalty and dedication. Trusting the associates is a precondition to their empowerment and engagement, and therefore a critical factor in achieving and sustaining total quality work performance.

An essential part of integrity of relationship deals with treating associates fairly. This begins with clearly stated expectations concerning the quantity, quality and timeliness of work outputs. There is nothing so unfair to an associate as not giving her/him clear expectations upon which the work generated will be evaluated. The same spirit of fairness urges leaders to offer opportunities for personal and professional growth through the work assignments. It calls for leaders who know their people and the abilities they possess, and at the same time, to help the associates advance their careers.

Probably the area in which this aspect of integrity most has its expression is in the organization's performance appraisal system. Fair and equitable treatment of associates begins with the statement of clear expectations described earlier. The more the judgment of performance quality is based on objective measureable factors, the fairer the process will likely be, because subjective assessments are eliminated from the equation. Such objective measurements, evenly administered for all associates, provide a system that lends itself to fairness, and is likely to be perceived as such by the associates.

One of the aspects of the integrity of relationship with which nonprofit organizations struggle is fair compensation. Too often budgetary constraints are cited as a rationale for paying associates less than they deserve. Leaders of nonprofit organizations need to consult national and regional nonprofit salaries for comparable positions in comparable organizations to be aware of what the market values of the various positions are. In fairness, this data should be shared with the associate to determine where her/his position resides in the comparative salary scale. If the associate is a valued asset and the organization wishes to retain her/his services, but doesn't have the financial ability to increase the salary to reach the comparable position's average salary, a plan should be devised to demonstrate how, over a reasonable period of time, assuming continued excellent work performance, the salary will be increased. An effective leader will also connect this escalation process to continued organizational success.

Another area in which compensation practices fail the fairness test is in the difference between executive compensation and benefits and the other associates. The same type of national and regional comparative salary studies are available and should be consulted before offering a contract to a new executive or compensating an incumbent.

The compensation practice that most frequently fails the "fairness test" is the practice of offering the same "across the board" salary increases to everyone, regardless of performance. In this case the equitable treatment is actually unfair, and such practices should be avoided. These raises are often so small a percentage of salary to make an appreciable difference in take home pay. If there is a limited salary pool from which to award raises or bonuses, it needs to be spent proportionately on those whose performance warrants such treatment based on the level that their work effort contributed to the surplus pool.

Leaders need to ensure that their interpersonal relationships with associates always remains at the professional level. To this end, overly familiar fraternization outside of the work environment can easily lead observers to misinterpret the relationship between the leader and associate. Further, the leader's ability to maintain a professional objectivity toward the associate might be lessened or called into question. Despite how cold this may appear, it is actually fair to both the leader and the associate and removes any cause for suspicion or hurtful rumor mongering.

The customers enjoy a privileged priority in the organization committed to total quality. As such the organization's interactions with them should also be governed by an integrity of relationship. This begins with truth in advertising. The quality nonprofit whose leadership exhibits an integrity of relationship will set clear ethical standards for the marketing and sales professionals. Since this area is so critical to total quality, it is recommended that the Marketing and Sales team report directly to the President. If this is not practical or feasible, then it is important for the President to set clear ethical standards for promoting and selling the organization's offerings and the organization itself, and to regularly ensure that the standards are being met.

Integrity of relationship should govern an organization's pricing structure. The goal should be to price an organization's offerings on the *fair price* principle, rather than what the market will bear, or beyond a reasonable return on investment. Almost every nonprofit has its "cash cows", and while the reasons for these are usually reasonable and practical, they should not violate the fair pricing principle. Nonprofits exist to serve a *public interest*. The pricing of their offerings should support this purpose. To the extent that pricing becomes a deterrent to easy and universal access, it can no longer be considered fair or appropriate for a nonprofit.

Again, many nonprofits sponsor fund raising events whose pricing and nature are obviously not designed for the organization's general public. These events teeter on a very precarious line between the organization's mission and unfair pricing practices for a nonprofit. Care needs to be taken by the organization's leadership that the line is not crossed by these events because of the limited access generated through their pricing.

Integrity of action calls for leaders to act with the courage of their convictions, and in support of the nobility of their organization's missions. Integrity of action gives a sense of comfort to the espousal of the leaders' personal and organizational principles, and the strength of purpose to base their actions and decisions upon them. This is particularly significant for those in leadership positions, because they are the spokespersons and "public faces" of the organizations they represent.

But more important than the leaders' words are the leaders' deeds. Integrity of action is most often reflected in the everyday life of an organization in the the decisions leaders make. First of all, integrity of action should impel and inspire leaders to make decisions, and that these decisions should be consistent with the principles governing the operations of a total quality organization: mission driven, customer satisfaction, continuous improvement, and collegiality. Secondly, but no less important, decisions should also reflect the best practices of personal and professional ethics.

Much has been said throughout the book with regard to the efficacy of the consultative process in decision making and the benefit of teams. While these are indeed conditions for optimal operational performance, they should in no way be construed as impediments to, or replacements for effective decision making. Leaders should involve others in the process of decision making, but leaders should never relinquish their right and responsibility to make the final decisions. Teams advise, leaders govern. The quality of the leaders' decisions will be enhanced through a consultative process, but this process must be clearly defined and maintained as consultative.

Integrity of action requires leaders to consider carefully the advice rendered as a result of the consultative process, and more often, than not, make the final decision based on the advice proffered. In situations that this is not possible, leaders should discuss the reasons why the final decision cannot match the advice given.

There are decisions that leaders have to make that should not and cannot be subject to a consultative process, such as staff reductions or downsizing of departments. These moments require courage which is the virtue most associated with integrity of action. While these decisions may not be made with associate involvement in a consultative process, integrity of action calls for them to be objectively arrived at through objective analysis of available data, rather than any more subjective judgments.

Another example of integrity of action is the leaders' ability to offer an apology. Often apologizing is seen by some in leadership positions as weakness. To the contrary, there are few moments that display the leader's courage and integrity more than the sincerely offered and genuinely meant apology. These apologies must have as their sole objective the rectifying of an error or the resolution of a personal or professional offense taken. Political posturing only serves to add to the offense and certainly lacks integrity. Apologies that are offered in a simple, direct and personal manner are most effective for resolving any long term impact of the cause. The temptation to offer excuses or explanations as part of the apology should be resisted; they weaken the apology's strength and very often will sound defensive, even argumentative and for these reasons must be eschewed.

Mistakes will be made, it is the way of human organizations. Even in high performing organizations there will be times that through no malice of intent, mistakes will be made by individuals or by the organization as a whole, or actions taken with the best of intentions, will be misinterpreted. Quality organizations will admit to these mistakes and at the same time reinforce the continuous improvement efforts that will be initiated to guarantee that the mistake will not occur again.

Throughout this discussion about the leadership characteristic of integrity it is clear that quality organizations must subscribe to the practices outlined in the exercise of integrity of character, relationship, and action. Quality organizations deserve no less.

Concluding Thoughts

There are two other characteristics that leaders of quality organizations must possess and exhibit in the performance of their responsibilities: patience and a sense of humor.

It is evident from all that has been discussed throughout the book that the continuous improvement thrust that drives the total quality organization requires its leadership to understand that the changes that are endemic to continuous improvement will not be realized in an instant or "overnight". Their full realization and impact will take time, and therefore, the need for the leadership to exhibit reasonable patience. It is further evident that total quality organizations are committed to the empowerment and engagement of their associates and the use of cross functional teams in the development, implementation and assessment of the organization's offerings. Results generated through teamwork will take longer to execute, but, by and large, will be worth the wait in terms of their quality and support.

It must be obvious by now that to lead a nonprofit committed to total quality will be hard work. The demands placed upon the organization and its leadership are many and great. The intensity of its operations and the constant striving for continuous improvement and customer satisfaction will create at times a very stressful environment. It is imperative that the organization's leaders maintain a balance of perspective, and above all, a sense of humor that affords the leaders to ability to laugh at themselves and their own intensity and foibles, and in like manner, those of their colleagues. This will go a long way to keeping an objective frame of reference and a healthy sense of balance.

Patience and a sense of humor and the corresponding personal balance they generate in leaders will provide sustenance and perspective for the leaders.

Ultimately, each nonprofit must make the intentional decision to be an organization committed to total quality. The theories and practices described herein are clear indications of the ways and means to accomplish that goal. Some may argue that it is too demanding a task and shrink from the effort, or choose only some aspects of the process. It is hoped that many will choose the "road less travelled" and commit to the full process. It is hard work, but the end state for the organization can exceed one's wildest imaginings.

The organizations that will succeed in developing and sustaining a culture committed to total quality will have leaders who possess and demonstrate the characteristics developed above. They are enthused about the inherent challenges themselves, and infuse the organization with a realistic, not fanciful, *sense of possibility* that the organization's dreams can be fulfilled and they can be, and will be, realized through the hard work of all.

The decision that each nonprofit organization will make in determining its desire and commitment to total quality is the choice between surviving or excelling as an organization. It is indeed nothing less than the decision ***TO BE THE BEST!***

APPENDICES

Appendix 1
SWOT Analysis Sample

Organization:

Instructions: *Please list your* **honest** *impressions/ perceptions of the organization named above for each of the areas below. Assessments may be made on any and all aspects of the organization. Areas to be considered, but not limited to, are: governance, staffing, services, programming, marketing/promotion, finances, fund raising...*

STRENGTHS: *What internal aspect(s) serve to ensure consistent quality performance and mission fulfillment?*

WEAKNESSES: *What internal aspect(s) render the organization ineffective to perform at its maximum potential, or what aspect(s) place the organization at a competitive disadvantage?*

OPPORTUNITIES: *What current condition(s) or possible future condition(s) in the external environment might give the organization a better competitive advantage or opportunity for growth?*

THREATS: *What conditions in the external environment might put the organization* at a competitive disadvantage and/or inhibit achievement of its mission or the ability to deliver quality services and/or threaten its very existence?

Please return the completed form in a sealed envelope to the address below by DATE

Contact Person
Organization Name
Organization Address

THANK YOU FOR YOUR PARTICIPATION

Appendix 2
SWOT Analysis Cover Letter Sample

Date

Name
Address 1
Address 2

Dear .

The Board of Directors of the **ORGANIZATION'S NAME** is engaged in a strategic planning process. It is being coordinated by **CO/CHAIRS NAMES**. We invite your participation in the process by completing the enclosed instrument that seeks to identify the organization's strengths, weaknesses, opportunities and threats (SWOT). Specific instructions for the completion and return of completed forms are included in the instrument.

If you have engaged in a strategic planning process before you know the value of this type of input. It is our very strong hope that you will take the few minutes required to complete the form with your honest impressions and perceptions of the organization.

The analysis is to be completed anonymously. All individual responses will only be seen by the contact person listed below and held in confidence by her/him. She/he will prepare a summary document for the board's review, but in no way will that summary identify any individual participant's responses.

Completed analyses are to be sent directly in a sealed envelope no later than *DATE* to:

CONTACT NAME
CONTACT ADDRESS

My fellow Board members join me in thanking you for your anticipated participation. Your input and insights are greatly valued and appreciated.

Sincerely yours,

Board Chairperson

Appendix 3
Board Assessment Instrument

ORGANIZATION'S NAME:

Please review the following aspects of your Board membership during the past year. This is designed to be a self-administered exercise; its results are for your information and benefit only.

PARTICIPATION:

In the past year...

- How many of the regularly scheduled board meetings have I attended?
- How many committee meetings have I attended?
- Have I regularly attended the organization's fund raising and promotional events?
- How engaged have I been in the discussions at the meetings I attended?
- What, if any, improvements can I make in my participation for next year?

ADVISORY:

In the past year...

- How often have I offered my counsel, advice and expertise to the organization and its staff?
- Are there ways that this role can be improved?

FUND RAISING:

In the past year...

- Have I made an annual gift to the organization to the level at which I am able?
- Have I encouraged others to support the organization through an annual gift?
- What, if any, improvements can I make in the fund raising aspect of my board membership for next year?

PROMOTION:

In the past year...

- How strongly have I advocated for the organization and its good works?
- How often have I shared the organization's value and benefit with professional colleagues? Personal friends?
- Are there areas in the promotional expectation that I can improve?.

OVERALL RATING:

Based on your evaluation of the four areas above, please rate the quality of your board membership for the past year? (5 outstanding; 4 excellent; 3 good; 2 some areas need improvement; 1 poor) _____

Appendix 4
Candidate Assessment Form

CANDIDATE'S NAME _____

Please evaluate the candidate listed above. Please be as candid as possible; if you need more space, feel free to use the back of the page.

What are the candidate's strengths?

What are the candidate's weaknesses?

What risk does the organization face if this person is selected as President?

What is your overall rating of this candidate?

Superior _____ Very Good _____ Good _____
Poor _____ Not to be Considered _____

Thank you for your participation. Please return the completed form to: (Contact person's name and mailing address.) no later than (date).

Appendix 5
Candidate Finalist Rating System

CANDIDATE		1	2	3
Length of Experience	(5)	2 (10)	3 (15)	1 (5)
Relevance of Experience	(4)	1 (4)	3 (12)	2 (8)
Professional Demeanor	(3)	2 (6)	1 (3)	3 (9)
Presentation Skills	(2)	3 (6)	1 (2)	2 (4)
Educational Credentials	(1)	3 (3)	1 (1)	2 (2)
TOTALS		(29)	(33)	(28)

Candidate 3 is the choice based on the ranking & weighting of the criteria.

Appendix 6
Needs Assessment Template

ORGANIZATION:

POPULATION: Composite (All Management & Supervisors)   *n*=26

Item	Freq.	Rank	# 1	Item	Freq.	Rank	# 1
Change Mgt.	3	2.33	1	Negotiation	N/A	N/A	N/A
Communication	14	2.41	5	Perf. Appraisal	8	3,62	2
Conflict Resolution	12	3.99	1	Proj. Mgt.	7	2.72	0
Corp. Cult. Analysis	N/A	N/A	N/A	Prof. Ethics	3	3.25	0
Customer Serv.	9	2.58	2	Presentation Skills	4	3.50	0
Empowering Empl.	10	3.25	0	Quality Mgt.	10	1.83	3
Group Dynamics	1	2.00	0	Sales Techniques	N/A	N/A	N/A
Innovation	7	3.83	0	Team Mgt.	11	2.662	6
Leadership/Styles	12	2.88	3	Time Mgt.	7	2.86	2
Meeting Facilitation	N/A	N/A	N/A				
Motivation	12	3.61	3	Other: N/A			

TOP THREE BY FREQUENCY:	TOP THREE BY MEAN RANK:	TOP THREE BY # 1 RANKING:
COMMUNICATION	QUALITY MANAGEMENT	TEAM MANAGEMENT
CONFLICT RESOLUTION ***	CHANGE MANAGEMENT	COMMMUNICATION
MOTIVATION ***	COMMUNICATION	LEADERSHIP & LEAD STYLES ***
LEADERSHIP & LEAD. STYLES ***		MOTIVATION ***
		QUALITY MANAGEMENT ***

*** Tied

Appendix 7
Customer Satisfaction Template

Organization:

Program/Event/Performance:

Date:

It is our goal to consistently delight our customers by offering them quality offerings. Your input into this process is critical and important to us. Please take a few minutes to complete the questionnaire below and return the completed form to (place) upon leaving. We appreciate you and your support.

Please circle the number that best describes your level of satisfaction:

1. Very dissatisfied
2. Dissatisfied
3. Satisfied
4. Very Satisfied

In the space below please share with us your reason(s) for the ranking:

_____

_____

Thank You.

BIBLIOGRAPHY

Blanchard, Ken. Leading At A Higher Level. (Englewood Cliffs, NJ: Prentice Hall) 2007

Champy, James. Reengineering Management: The Mandate for New Leadership. (New York, NY: Harper-Collins Publishers Inc.) 1995

Drucker, Peter F. Managing the Nonprofit Organization. (New York, NY: Harper-Collins Publishers Inc.) 1990

Evans, James R. Quality & Performance Excellence. (Mason. OH: South-Western Cengage Learning) 2011

French, W.L., & Bell C.H. Organizational Development: Behavioral Interventions for Organizational Improvement. (Englewood Cliffs, NJ: Prentice Hall) 1978

Herman, Robert D., & Heimovics, Richard D. Executive Leadership in Nonprofit Organizations. (San Francisco, CA: Jossey-Bass Publishers) 1991

Hersey, Paul, Blanchard, Kenneth H., & Johnson, Dewey E. Management of Organizational Behavior. (Upper Saddle River, NJ: Pearson Ed. Inc.) 2008

Houle, Cyril O. Governing Boards. (San Francisco, CA: Jossey-Bass Publishers) 1989

Hughes, Richard L. & Beatty Colarelli, Katherine. Becoming a Strategic Leader. (San Francisco CA: John Wiley & Sons, Inc.) 2005

Kotter, J.P. Leading Change. (Boston, MA: Harvard Business School Press) 1996

Kreitner, Robert, & Kinichi, Angelo. Organizational Behavior. (New York, NY: McGraw Hill Irwin) 2010

Lowney, Chris. Heroic Leadership. (Chicago, IL: Loyola Press) 2003

Michaud, Thomas A. The Virtue of Business Ethics. (Acton, MA: Copley Custom Textbooks) 2010

Morris, Tom. If Aristotle Ran General Motors. (New York, NY: Henry Holt & Co) 1997